What Others Are Saying about
Unmasking the

"Most believers I know have fallen into these deadly traps of slander, gossip, and offense. *Unmasking the Accuser* will stop the devil in his tracks and free you from a lifetime of diminished vision, anointing, and destiny."
—*Sid Roth*
Host, *It's Supernatural!*

"Kynan Bridges has a wonderful ability to articulate biblical truth. He gets straight to the point, deals with the thorniest of issues, and applies God's remedy. *Unmasking the Accuser* is no exception as it exposes the root of so many issues and snares that rob us of victory. Read this practical book, receive the truth, and get ready to walk in a new level of freedom and power!"
—*Aliss Cresswell*
Director, Spirit Lifestyle and Morning Star Europe

"Why be duped by the devil? Dr. Kynan Bridges' book does a powerful job of unmasking the Accuser—Satan. You will be amazed by what the devil's been up to in your life and in your church! This book is an incredible tool for fighting the 'nice' sins inside the church that cause such division: slander, gossip, and offense. With kingdom authority and pastoral power, *Unmasking the Accuser* shows the danger of lending an ear to evil and shows the blessing of choosing Christ instead. The revelation in this book will expose Satan, challenge believers—and change your life!"
—*Bishop George G. Bloomer*
Best-selling author, *Witchcraft in the Pews*
Author, *Break Loose*
Pastor, Bethel Family Worship Center
Durham, NC

"*Unmasking the Accuser* discloses the subtle tactics that our enemy, the Accuser, deliberately uses to destroy us. Dr. Kynan Bridges provides a strategic plan to take back what you have lost in your authority and evict the Accuser permanently from your life. It is a powerful addition to your reference library."

—*Cindy Stewart*
Author, *7 Visions, Believing God,* and *Believing His Word*
Pastor, The Gathering with Jesus
Tarpon Springs, FL

"God has given my friend, Kynan Bridges, profound insight into the enemy's greatest weapon against you. In *Unmasking the Accuser*, Kynan exposes those nagging voices of insecurity, offense, guilt, and shame for what they really are—devices of the devil designed to steal your destiny. Get ready to experience restoration, healing, and freedom! Through in-depth teaching and powerful application, you'll learn how to recognize, combat, and silence Satan's slander to finally live in the victory of the Voice of Truth!"

—*Kyle Winkler*
Author, Activating the Power of God's Word
Creator, Shut Up, Devil! App
www.kylewinkler.org

"I believe that Pastor Kynan Bridges' new book, *Unmasking the Accuser*, actually provides the key that will help the church sustain the Holy Spirit outpouring she has long prayed and talked about. It has little to do with God sovereignly sending something from heaven; it has everything to do with being positioned to effectively steward the move of God, from generation to generation. Why do we see trickles of outpouring when Jesus prophesied of rivers? Simple. Because we've been called to direct the fight at the powers of darkness, not at each other. *Unmasking the Accuser* shines light on Satan's favorite lie that, in my opinion, has crippled revival, destroyed churches, and paralyzed people from fulfilling their personal destinies. It's that big of a deal. Pastor Kynan does a fantastic job at breaking down the different strategies of the devil and, ultimately, exposing the enemy's timeless playbook. My prayer is this: that you would not read this like just another book, but you would literally act like, somehow, the devil's handbook of age-old strategies has been placed in your possession. Imagine having exclusive insider knowledge of the key tactics that the enemy of your soul plans to use against you. *Unmasking the Accuser* provides you with that! As you read it, I trust that you will start anticipating the devil's next move and have the winning advantage over his weapons of offense, gossip, slander, and deception!"

—*Larry Sparks*
Vice-president, Destiny Image
Author, *Breakthrough Faith*
lawrencesparks.com

"I first met Dr. Kynan Bridges when we each appeared as a guest on the same popular Christian television program. I came to recognize that Kynan is smart, articulate, charismatic, attentive, and humble. He's obviously anointed, but he's also a man who loves the Lord and genuinely cares about people. That day I was also blessed to get one of his books, and as I read it I found that in addition to all that, he's a gifted writer. I really liked that first book—and I really like this one! I believe *Unmasking the Accuser* will help you order your everyday conversation to glorify God, and will also help you to avoid or recover from hurts you may have sustained through the hurtful words of others. I would go so far as to say it's a must-read for every Christian. In these pages Kynan reveals the destructive power of slander, gossip, and offense, and shows us all how to avoid being stuck in their claws. As you read, take Kynan's powerful teaching to heart, and be set free in every way!"

—*Karen J. Salisbury*
Author, *How to Make the Right Decision Every Time*
and *Why God Why?*
www.karenjsalisbury.org

"*Unmasking the Accuser* is a book that exposes the enemy for the liar that he is. Through honest and insightful teaching, Dr. Bridges helps believers identify the voice of the enemy in their lives and invites the reader to live in the truth of who they are in Christ. I encourage you to read this book and personalize the prayers within that you may shut the mouth of the enemy over your life, hear God's voice with clarity, and live out His truth with conviction!"

—*Katherine Ruonala*
Katherine Ruonala Ministries
www.katherineruonala.com

UNMASKING
THE ACCUSER

UNMASKING
THE ACCUSER

HOW TO FIGHT SATAN'S **FAVORITE LIE**

KYNAN BRIDGES

WHITAKER
HOUSE

All definitions of Greek words are taken from the New Testament Greek Lexicon—King James Version, based on Thayer and Smith's Bible Dictionary, plus others (public domain), www.BibleStudyTools.com. All definitions of Hebrew words are taken from the Old Testament Hebrew Lexicon—King James Version, which is the Brown, Driver, Briggs, Gesenius Lexicon (public domain), www.BibleStudyTools.com.

Unless otherwise marked, Scripture quotations are taken from the *King James Version Easy Read Bible*, KJVER®, © 2001, 2007, 2010, 2015 by Whitaker House. Used by permission. All rights reserved. Scripture quotations marked (ESV) are taken from *The Holy Bible, English Standard Version*, © 2000, 2001, 1995 by Crossway Bibles, a division of Good News Publishers. Used by permission. All rights reserved.

Boldface type in the Scripture quotations indicates the author's emphasis.

All definitions taken from *OxfordDictionaries.com*, Oxford University Press, © 2015.

UNMASKING THE ACCUSER:
How to Fight Satan's Favorite Lie

Kynan Bridges Ministries, Inc.
P. O. Box 159
Ruskin, FL 33575
www.kynanbridges.com
info@kynanbridges.com

ISBN: 978-1-62911-808-6
eBook ISBN: 978-1-62911-809-3
Printed in the United States of America
© 2017 by Kynan Bridges

Whitaker House
1030 Hunt Valley Circle
New Kensington, PA 15068
www.whitakerhouse.com

Library of Congress Cataloging-in-Publication Data (Pending)

1 2 3 4 5 6 7 8 9 10 11 ⨀ 24 23 22 21 20 19 18 17

DEDICATION

I dedicate this book to the Lord Jesus Christ,
the King of Kings and Lord of Lords.
I also dedicate it to Gloria Bridges—my lovely, awesome, and
virtuous wife, the mother of my four children,
and my number-one partner and supporter in life and ministry;
I love you more than words can express.
And I dedicate it to all those who have been hurt by the church.
My prayer is that you will find healing and restoration in the
pages of this work.
God bless!

CONTENTS

FOREWORD

As a veteran to spiritual warfare, prayer, and the revelatory ways of God, the contents of this book are things I teach. So I am thrilled to see another voice, another person of high character, a person in another sphere, teaching what I would teach. Yes! This book is filled with practical, relatable, and inspirational tools to help you grow and mature in your walk with God.

No matter who you are, no matter where you live, no matter what you do, God is speaking down to you. Now He is saying many things, things that shape and change our world, but think first simply about that grace-filled fact: *God is speaking to you!* It's not just the *things* He whispers to our hearts, it's *that* He whispers to our hearts and transforms us into lovers of Him. When we hold this knowledge close as we go about our day, listening for His voice, we quietly perform one part of the lost art of practicing His presence. We watch grace grow. Love. Perseverance. Gentleness.

But God is not the only one speaking to you. His is not the only voice in your ear. Hundreds of other voices swirl around us demanding our attention and often pulling us down.

We all know it, if we're honest. Instead of leaning back into the sure sway of the Spirit, we find ourselves lending an ear to things we shouldn't. Backbiting. Pettiness. Gossip. Complaining. If you've been around Christians, you unfortunately know exactly what I'm talking about. Who among us hasn't been in a situation where words caused wounding beyond comprehension? In my years of ministry through God Encounters Ministries, I have seen it over and over. So where does all this wounding come from?

The answer is more uncomfortable than most of us are willing to admit. More personal than we want to confront. My friend Dr. Kynan Bridges masterfully speaks a word of truth over the discord and disunity seeping into the precious body of God-followers by demonstrating that when we lend an ear to slander and gossip, we are welcoming in the serpent of old, who is the devil and Satan. He is the one planting accusations and deceit inside our minds through the lips of even well-meaning people! *The devil uses our words to wound.* What a wake-up call!

Words are powerful, powerful as a double-edged sword, and we can either use them for great good or for great harm. If we're not careful, we can wreak havoc with our words, especially when from one mouth proceeds both blessing and cursing. (See James 3:10.) The words we listen to affect the words we speak, and the words we speak affect every single person who crosses our path. That's why *Unmasking the Accuser* is a desperately needed prophetic book for us today, with the potential to radically change every single word spoken in our lives—impacting our eternal destinies.

I encourage you to take the words of this book and let them shine a bright light of clarity into the conversations of your life, as they have shone into mine.

If we are to passionately pursue the fire of the Spirit, we must lay aside every voice but His. It will take discernment: Sometimes, our heavenly Father speaks through the words of the people around us. And, as Dr. Bridges wrote, "Sometimes Satan speaks in the first person." But this book will be your guide to unmasking the powerful lies that come from the mouth of devil and discerning the truth that comes from the mouth of God. Instead of letting lies in the front door of our mind, let us participate in a great, international, supernatural conversation that flows forth the words of our holy God, not the words of the Accuser of the brethren.

Imagine how much less slander, gossip, and offense there would be in our lives—in our world! Imagine the joy of our Creator as He would watch us spread blessings and transformational power instead of cursing and stagnating criticism. Imagine the healing, reparation, and reconciliation that would spring up in the hearts of believers. I am excited about this book. Can you tell?

Once again let us be the sweet fragrance of Christ to all the nations. Speak life!

—*Dr. James W. Goll*
Founder, God Encounters Ministries
Author, *Hearing God's Voice Today,*
The Seer, Passionate Pursuit, and others

PREFACE

Slander, gossip, and offense.

I call them the devil's trio.

I have counseled thousands of people who are bound by these three debilitating forces. Slander, gossip, and offense have affected countless people in the world at large and in the church in particular. Maybe you have been slandered by a loved one, been the victim of gossip, or been hurt within the church community. Or maybe you have been the perpetrator of such behavior. Regardless, God wants you to enjoy freedom like you have never experienced before.

But, I have hard news for you: this journey will require honesty. Honesty with God and honesty with yourself. In the pages of this book we will unmask the Accuser for who he really is: a liar who desires to see you and me bitter, broken, and defeated. We will expose the destructive power of slander, gossip, and offense, and learn how to avoid getting trapped in their claws. We will discern the deceptive and insidious tactics the enemy tries to use to manipulate you out of your God-ordained destinies. You will receive powerful biblical keys that will help you to heal from the wounds of past hurts and offenses.

My prayer is that the Holy Spirit will speak to you clearly and powerfully on every page!

ACKNOWLEDGMENTS

First of all, I want to take a moment and acknowledge my precious Lord Jesus Christ. It is through Him that I am able to write this and all books. To my wife—you mean more than life itself. Thank you for standing with me through the years. To my ministerial staff, thank you! To my church family (Grace & Peace Global Fellowship), who have been instrumental in praying for and supporting this project—thank you! To the team at Whitaker House—thank you for your hard work and prayerful support in helping to get this message to the world: I am grateful for all that you do. Special thanks to the production and editing team, including Christine Whitaker, Judith Dinsmore, and Cathy Hickling at Whitaker; Crystal Dixon, Patricia Holdsworth, Camilla Hippolyte, Gloria Bridges, and the entire Kynan Bridges Ministries Team, to name a few.

I also want to take a moment to acknowledge great men and women of the faith who have impacted my life and ministry in a positive way (either directly or indirectly), including: Pastor Wayne C. Thompson, Dr. Mark Chironna, John G. Lake, Derek Prince, Dr. Charles Stanley, Oswald Chambers, Smith Wigglesworth, John Wesley, Jack Coe, Oral Roberts, Kathryn Kuhlman, R.W. Shambach, Sid Roth, Pastor Marlin D. Harris, Mike Bickle, Hank and Brenda Kunneman, Joan Hunter, Dr. E. V. Hill, Marilyn Hickey, Pastor Tony Kemp, Dr. Douglas Wingate, Evangelist Reinhard Bonnke, Dr. Rodney Howard-Browne, Dr. T. L. Lowery, and Dr. Myles Munroe.

I

WHO'S IN YOUR EAR?

Now the serpent was more subtle than any beast of the field which the LORD God had made. And he said to the woman, Yea, has God said, You shall not eat of every tree of the garden? (Genesis 3:1)

Her eyes were sparkling with interest, amazement, and suspense. Her face was covered in anticipation. Her hand was clutching the forbidden fruit. As she wrestled with the inner conflict of good and evil, right and wrong, her next decision would determine her fate and the fate of the entire human race. And with one bite, everything changed.

As she handed the fruit to her husband, she realized that something had gone very wrong. Suspense turned into suspicion, and anticipation turned into shame. *"What have I done?"* Sudden knowledge flooded her being: this sin had cost her more than she was prepared to pay and taken her further than she was willing to go.

Can you see the look on Eve's face when she ate from the Tree of the Knowledge of Good and Evil? Can you imagine the betrayal that she felt as a result of transgressing God's law? Can you feel the embarrassment that ensued when she realized that the taste of the fruit was not worth the cost of her future—the cost of her life? And all of this was the result of one little conversation that dishonored her Creator!

That is not just the story of Adam and Eve's fate in the garden of Eden. It is also the story of Satan's favorite lie. So many believers have fallen for this lie, time and again, that the story of the church has begun to sound like a broken record. Countless, like Adam and Eve, accept a narrative from the enemy that robs them of their peace of mind, their joy, and even their future, as they run to embrace the lie that real knowledge can be found outside of God. The lie that it's OK to listen to any voice other than His. The lie that lending an ear to the Accuser's slander and gossip, letting it boil into offense, is somehow innocent and harmless.

The real truth is, *the conversation you give ear to can cost you everything.*

Eve and the Serpent

The plague of slander, gossip, offense, and bitterness cannot be solved overnight because it did not happen overnight. It began long before you and I were aware of its devastation; it began with the first man and woman on the planet. The beginning of the biblical account of humankind's fall is a little conversation between Eve and the Serpent.

> *Now the serpent was more subtle than any beast of the field which the* LORD *God had made. And he said to the woman, Yea, has God said, You shall not eat of every tree of the garden?*

The word *serpent* here comes from the Hebrew word *nachash*, which can also mean "divination." The conversation the Serpent (the devil) had with Eve was much more than a conversation. The Serpent was hissing a *divination* into Eve's ear, tempting her to seek knowledge of good and evil, of future and unknown things, by supernatural means. In other words, Eve was being seduced into seeking knowledge, wisdom, and insight outside of the confines of God's will. She was beguiled into believing that she was missing some very pertinent information concerning the happiness of her life. The Serpent was inviting her into territory that was outside of her jurisdiction and manipulating her expectations and her desires. God never made it Eve's business to know her future. It was her responsibility to know God's instruction, and it was God's responsibility to steward her future. But she wanted what God had. She wanted to know what God knew!

The Bible also tells us that the Serpent was subtle. This is the Hebrew word *aruwm*, which means "shrewd, crafty, and sly." This was never an innocent conversation, but a diabolical attempt to remove Adam and Eve from their position in the garden of Eden.

SATAN'S LIE: YOU'RE NOT AFFECTED BY WHAT YOU HEAR.
#WHOSINYOUREAR?

Have you ever wondered why Eve spoke to the Serpent to begin with? Why did she allow him to speak into her life? You've heard the saying, "Curiosity killed the cat." Well in this case, curiosity brought the curse. She allowed the words the Serpent spoke to her to overrule the instructions God had given. What you hear is fundamental to your spiritual life because it is directly attached to your faith. Faith brings manifestation; whatever you accept into your ears will determine what you act upon in your life. What you hear will always work for you or against you, depending on what you let in. It will affect you, both in its quality and its quantity.

So who is in your ear? You need to know this: Satan, the devil, is a liar. He has been a liar from the beginning, and is incapable of speaking the truth. He is not a credible source of information because nothing he says is truthful, including what he says about you, and what he says to you. Do not lend your ear to the enemy!

Every time we allow the wrong voice to speak into our ears, it costs us something. When Eve listened, it cost her God's glory, her peace of mind, and mankind's position as vice-regents in the earth. Words are seeds, and Eve realized the hard way that every seed produces a harvest.

The Subtleness of Slander

Maybe you never looked at it this way, but the first transgression recorded in the Bible is not the eating of forbidden fruit; it is slander. *Slander* is defined as the action or crime of making a false spoken statement damaging to a person's reputation. Whose reputation was being assaulted? Who was the first victim of this slander? God! The devil spoke lies about God in an attempt to malign His character in the eyes of Eve. The enemy of her soul wanted her to believe that God was not telling her the whole story. He wanted her to think that God was hiding something from her. In fact, the word for *Satan* (*shatan*) literally means, "one who breaks faith."

He slithered up to Eve and with his first words insinuated that God had made a ridiculous request. "**Yea***, has God said, You shall not eat of* **every tree** *of the garden?*" "*Yea*" implies, "Indeed, is it really true?" and notice that he says, "*every tree.*" Now, I'll bet anything that Satan knew exactly what the rule was, but he subtly slandered God by making Him out to be a mean old guy with a garden full of beautiful fruit trees who won't even share *one*.

After Eve responds that they were only forbidden from eating of the Tree of the Knowledge of Good and Evil, the Serpent becomes bolder. He directly contradicts God in order to cast suspicion on God's intentions and cause Eve to doubt. "*You shall not surely die,*" said the Serpent. The moment she took heed to this slanderous accusation against God, her spiritual eyes were darkened and she became deceived.

OUR CONVERSATIONS SHAPE OUR PERCEPTIONS, AND OUR PERCEPTIONS SHAPE OUR REALITY.

Have you ever looked at someone differently because of a conversation? Maybe someone told you something about a sister or brother in your church, and now you don't see him or her through the same innocent eyes anymore. Jesus said, "*Take heed what you hear: with what measure you mete, it shall be measured to you: and to you that hear shall more be given*" (Mark 4:24). Eve didn't heed—and now she wasn't seeing God through the same innocent eyes anymore, and neither would the rest of humankind.

The Sway of Gossip

Talking with Satan is never a good idea, unless you're using Jesus' words: "Get behind me, Satan." (See Matthew 16:23.) When Eve started chatting with the Serpent, she was opening the door to all kinds of evil. At first she corrected him—"*We may eat of the fruit of the trees of the garden*" (Genesis 3:2)—but then she let the Serpent rub off on her a little. The Serpent had exaggerated the rules, and now Eve does too: "*But of the fruit of the tree which is in the midst of the garden, God has said, You shall not eat of it, **neither shall you touch it**, lest you die*" (verse 3). God never said not to touch it! Maybe Eve was just being extra cautious. But I think something else is happening here. She is buying Satan's lie that God is a mean old guy. *He won't even let us touch the fruit!* she thinks.

SATAN'S LIE:
MAYBE GOD'S NOT RIGHT.
#WHOSINYOUREAR?

Now, it might seem a stretch to call this gossip, and, yes, it does look different from the gabfests in the grocery store. But there's one important similarity here: Eve and the Serpent are casually talking about God and misrepresenting Him when they think He's not in the room. Sounds like gossip to me! Slander and gossip opened the door to an alternative narrative, an alternate opinion. *Maybe God isn't right*, Eve thought.

The moment she heeded the voice of the devil, her opinion became more important than what God said. As a result of broken confidence in the character of God, Eve no longer trusted His Word and no longer saw the need to keep His commandments.

> *And when the woman saw that the tree was good for food, and that it was pleasant to the eyes, and a tree to be desired to make one wise, she took of the fruit thereof, and did eat, and gave also to her husband with her; and he did eat.* (Genesis 3:6)

What changed? Why did the tree take on a different appeal than before? The answer is key to a very important spiritual principle: our conversations shape our perceptions, and our perceptions shape our reality. The moment Eve listened to the lies of the enemy, it changed the way she saw things. The conversations we entertain shape our worldview. This is why the Bible uses the term *divination* to describe what happened to Eve in the garden of Eden. She was under the bewitchment of the enemy. As she looked at the tree, she was allured by its beauty and succumbed to her desire to experience its bliss. Words affect how and what we see!

The problem, as is so often the problem with our opinions, is that her opinion was based on falsehood. The tree would not make them like gods! She was *already* created in the image and likeness of God. What the devil promised her was already in her possession!

More Than a Conversation

I think you can see that the conversation between the Serpent and Eve was more than just a conversation! It was a life-altering exchange. Something was deposited within Eve that would affect her marriage, her children, and every person that came into the world after her. There was an eternal significance to that conversation. It set rolling a chain of events that we're still living inside, and will until the return of Christ.

SATAN'S LIE:
IT'S JUST A CONVERSATION.
#WHOSINYOUREAR?

Now listen to me when I say that this exchange in the garden is not so different from the conversations *we* have day in and day out. What would happen if we realized that every conversation we engage in deposits something deep within us that could affect us for days, months, and maybe even years and generations afterward? Jesus meant what He said when He told us, *"Take heed what you hear"* (Mark 4:24).

When God created Adam, He made him a speaking spiritual being. Mankind was distinguished from every other species on the earth because of the ability to articulate thoughts in an intelligible way. Just as God created the physical world through words, mankind was given the power to communicate, and by so doing shape his environment. Words shape our world. God made it this way for a reason. This is why the things people say have such a profound effect on our lives. This is why slander and gossip are all tied up in our spiritual life, creating a web of lies, deceit, and destruction just like they did in the garden.

Merriam-Webster defines *conversation* as "an oral exchange of sentiments, observations, opinions, or ideas." It comes from the Old French word *conversation*, which means: "living together, having dealings with others, or the act of living with." What if you had to "live with" everything you conversed about? I can imagine Eve reflecting back hundreds of years later on the conversation she had with the Serpent, and what she would have done differently if she only knew what it would cost her.

Guard Your Heart!

The Bible admonishes us: *"Keep your heart with **all diligence**; for out of it are the issues of life"* (Proverbs 4:23). Simply put, the Bible is telling us to guard our hearts. Why is this so important? Before we answer that question, we must first understand what the *heart* really is. The heart is the seat of our deepest longings, desires, thoughts, affections, passions, and emotions. It is the place from which we exercise our will. This verse tells us that *"out of it [flow] the issues of life"*; this phrase means that the heart is literally an outsource, escape, or exit.

Have you ever been to a movie theater? I am sure the answer is yes. What you see on the big screen is a projection of what is transpiring inside the booth. There is a small movie reel that illustrates every scene of the movie. The projector displays this in magnified form on the screen in front of you.

Your heart is like that movie projector. It interprets experiences and broadcasts them into your consciousness, affecting your entire life. The narrative of the heart will determine the attitudes and actions of your life. In the natural world, everything that shows up on the movie reel will be projected onto the big screen. In the spiritual world, if pain, trauma, hurt, and disappointment are allowed to make their way on the film of your heart, they will be broadcasted in magnified form on the "big screen" of our lives. Essentially, whatever we allow into our heart will flow out of our heart as we interact with others.

This is why the Bible tells us to diligently guard what comes in through the ear gates and the eye gates. Everything we talk about affects our meditation, and everything we meditate upon gets into our hearts. Your meditation is your medication!

The problem is that we, like Eve, are very curious. All human beings have a deep susceptibility for interesting conversations about other people. Everywhere we look, there seems to be a juicy story about a recent scandal, or news of a dramatic love triangle, or a government cover-up being exposed. Unfortunately, the church has often followed the pattern of the world by producing what I call "Christian tabloids" that glory in exposing the same kind of drama within the circle of believers, just perhaps spiritualized. In my opinion, they are much worse than the secular tabloids because God has called the church to a higher standard than the world. He has called the church to His standard!

Every time we listen to something slanderous, negative, or defamatory about someone else, those words go deep into the recesses of our heart, and can potentially bring damage to our lives. The Bible says: *"The words of a talebearer are as wounds, and they go down into the innermost parts of the belly"* (Proverbs 18:8). The word "wound" literally implies something "burned into" our consciousness. In other words, you cannot un-hear something. Be careful when someone is trying to slander another person to you. Be careful when you read Christian tabloids that make their money off of the latest scandal or moral failure in the church. These things are designed to damage your heart and prevent you from seeing things with purity and grace. To be pure is to be free from contaminants and befoulment.

What if you believed that every conversation you have is a seed that will produce an exponential harvest? Would you continue having the same conversations? No one can truthfully say that negative conversations do not contaminate. Even if you are not the one who initiates a conversation, even if you are just a listener, that conversation can still have a dramatic effect upon your life and your future!

The Fruit Is Offense

Now, I know I said that this is a demonic trio, not a demonic couple. Slander and gossip inevitably result in a third evil: offense. And it is offense that is destroying the church from the inside out.

As a young believer, I was very impressionable. I assumed that everyone had my best interest at heart and that everyone in the church was in agreement with leadership. Why wouldn't they be? I found out the hard way that this is not always the case. At that time, I was actively involved in my church, and people knew it. One day a leader in the church told me that he wanted to meet with me after service. I was always happy to go to lunch with people in the church, and I really loved to eat. We went out and I was all excited.

But while I was sitting across from this minister enjoying our dinner, he began to say very negative things about the senior pastor. Apparently, he was offended by the senior pastor and was spreading this offense to me. I was so taken aback I didn't know what to say. I had a tremendous amount of respect for both individuals and I did not want to be argumentative. He knew that the things he said were really grieving me. I was confused, bewildered, and disappointed. Was he telling the truth? I did not see my senior pastor the way he was being portrayed in this conversation, but I also wanted to heed the words that were being spoken. The seeds of slander and gossip were fighting for space in my heart!

EVERY CONVERSATION IS A SEED THAT PRODUCES AN EXPONENTIAL HARVEST.

After a few more meetings with this minister, I felt a strong impression from the Lord to end the relationship and discontinue our meetings, and that is exactly what I did. Sadly, that particular person left the church and experienced much devastation in his personal life and ministry. Years later, he came back and apologized to the pastor for his actions. I am grateful that this pastor was eventually able to see the error of his ways and come to a place of reconciliation. From this experience, I learned a very valuable lesson. Be careful who and what you allow into your ears. What if slander and gossip had taken root in my heart? They would have produced the same fruit that was in the heart of this pastor: offense! That would have resulted in a downward spiral of my own! I believe that we can avoid the pitfalls of the enemy by taking stories such as these to heart.

You see, it's a deadly cycle. The natural cycle of a plant brings life: seeds grow into plants, the plants bear fruit which then drop seeds, and then a new plant grows from those seeds, and the cycle continues.

Slander and gossip also work in a cycle, but the cycle of these spirits brings death! Slander and gossip plant seeds in your heart, they grow and produce the fruit of offense and bitterness, and offense then spawns more slander and gossip in your heart and in the hearts of those around you.

There are no exceptions to this. None of us are exempt. All conversations sow seeds, whether good or evil, and evil conversations are destroying the church. We should learn the lesson from the garden of Eden that can potentially save us years of heartache, pain, and disappointment: don't listen to the devil!

For Discussion

1. How do our conversations affect our worldview?

2. If every conversation is a seed that produces an exponential harvest, what harvest will you be reaping from the conversations you had today? This week?

3. Every Christian, young and old, has to guard their hearts. How can you guard yours?

Testimony

A dear brother called me one day in distress. "Pastor, I want to inform you that I am leaving the church!" I was shocked because I thought all was going well with this man. "Why?" I quickly asked. "I am not getting along with a particular person," he responded.

As we began to talk, I realized that there was another issue underlying his desire to leave. Our conversation began to unmask the enemy's schemes. After an hour of talking on the phone, we both realized that the problem was not what it seemed to be. Most of it could have been summed up as a simple misunderstanding. With prayer and conversation we were able to fully rectify the problem. What would have happened if he had stormed out without knowing all the details or being able to speak about his grievance? A great situation would have been unnecessarily sabotaged. This is why it is so important for us to pray, communicate, and be willing to hear a different side of the story. Now this individual is a treasured member of our church.

Prayer

Father, in the name of Jesus, I thank You for Your truth. I thank You that You have enlightened my heart about the conversations we have. Just as I was given instruction from Your Word, I receive Your instruction to steer clear of the knowledge from Satan, the Serpent of old. I declare that my mind is the mind of Christ. I declare that the powers of slander, gossip, and offense are broken off of my life. I declare that my conversations are edifying and enriching. Father, I ask that You give me Your heart concerning this issue. Every seed in me that does not bring forth good fruit, I uproot it right now. These things I ask in the name of Your Son, Jesus Christ.

Amen.

2

ACCUSING THE ACCUSER

For we wrestle not against flesh and blood, but against principalities, against powers, against the rulers of the darkness of this world, against spiritual wickedness in high places. (Ephesians 6:12)

Let me ask you a serious question: Has someone who professed to be a Christian ever offended you? Have you ever experienced hurt or disappointment in the church community? Has someone in the choir, on the deacon committee, or from the pulpit deeply offended you in some way? More than likely, the answer to all these questions is "yes!" We have all had our share of painful experiences both inside and outside of the four walls of the church. We often dismiss it by thinking, *well, we're all human, right?* But what if there is much more to this issue than the frailty of our humanity? What if there is something far more malevolent working behind the scenes?

Churches have been destroyed, families have been ruined, and leaders have been discredited all because of three simple words: slander, gossip, and offense. Yet no one ever really questions who is behind it, possibly because the tools are often people who seem above reproach, such as highly esteemed Christians.

Consider this: Who stands to gain from a church splitting, a pastor shamefully leaving the ministry, or a member of a church being shamed and disgraced? Who is really responsible for Christians keeping malice with one another or holding bitterness in their hearts toward someone who has wounded or abused them?

Once you discover the answers to these questions, you will look at things from a totally different vantage point, and your life will never be the same again. You will be empowered to see the truth from God's perspective. You will experience a level of freedom that you never fathomed was possible.

I know because it happened to me.

A Vision of the Accuser

One day, I had a vision that seemed like a dream. I saw two Christians in the parking lot of their local church. They were having what appeared to be a normal conversation with one another until I noticed something very peculiar: on each of their shoulders were demons. And every time one of them would speak to the other, the demon on that one's shoulder would vomit on the listener. It was awful! I asked God, "What are those?" He answered, "Slander!"

SLANDER IS THE SPIRITUAL VOMIT OF THE UNDERWORLD;
EVERY TIME WE ENTERTAIN IT,
WE BECOME CONTAMINATED BY IT!

The people in the vision had no clue that this was taking place. They just thought that these were normal thoughts and ideas in their heads about each other. They were completely oblivious to the fact that Satan was behind it all. When I came out of the vision, I understood that it represented what has been going in the church for years. I realized that in this disgusting way, Satan has victimized many in the body of Christ.

Satan is the Accuser of the brethren:

And I heard a loud voice saying in heaven, Now is come salvation, and strength, and the kingdom of our God, and the power of His

Christ: *for the accuser of our brethren is cast down, which accused them before our God day and night.* (Revelation 12:10)

The word *accuser* literally means "one who accuses before a judge." The enemy of our souls is perpetually accusing us before God. Every time we make a mistake or miss the mark, the enemy is there to point out our flaws and shortcomings to our heavenly Father. Like a skilled, deceitful lawyer, the devil stands in the courtroom of the universe, railing accusations against God's church.

Not only does he bring accusations against us to God, but he also brings accusations against the saints to one another. Just as it was illustrated in my vision, Satan whispers his sinister accusations in the ears of the saints on a regular basis, yet few discern this clandestine scheme. Instead, we just hear floating around in our heads, *Sister Betty didn't speak to you today!* Or, *the pastor was aiming his whole sermon at you.* Or, *why didn't the Johnson family invite you to lunch? Maybe they don't like you!*

SATAN'S LIE:
THE REST OF THE CHURCH
IS OUT TO GET YOU.
#ACCUSINGTHEACCUSER

We have all been guilty of hosting this hellacious nonsense in our minds at one point or another. However, it is time to get those thoughts out of our heads and send them back to the pit from whence they came! In the name of Jesus! God is about to snatch the covers off the devil once and for all!

The Accuser on the Job

Many years ago, a dear friend of mine shared a very vivid testimony with me about a difficult experience he went through in his church. I was very close to this individual, and so this account is personal for me. The ministry that this friend was active in underwent a church split, and although my friend maintained a great deal of respect for both the senior pastor and the pastor who broke away, it was a very difficult time. Church splits are never easy!

One person whom he considered a mentor left and joined the "other church," and he and his mentor stayed in touch. One Sunday, the young man didn't have a ride to church so he called this mentor to see if he could go to church with him. It was a choice between going to church or staying in his dormitory and eating Ramen noodles. He chose to go to church! His mentor came and picked him up and they went to church together that Sunday. It was a great service! That was the first and last time he ever visited this other church. In his mind, it was just a visit. God had not released him to go to another church and neither did he have the desire to do so.

But word got back to his pastor that the young man had joined the other church. His pastor didn't take that too well—and let the young man know as much! The young man was astonished. He never joined another church; he simply went to one service. How could someone make up such a thing?

Now, he understood that the pastor was hurt, was living through a devastating time, and obviously felt betrayed; after all, nearly half the members left the church. On the other hand, he was offended that lies were blatantly being spread around and that his pastor believed them.

So, who's at fault? The young man? The pastor? The person or persons spreading rumors? The answer is everyone and no one. The young man never once considered that it was really the *devil* who was behind all of this. You see, *he* was the one who sought to cast suspicion, break trust, and ruin relationships, even when no one was really at fault. The truth is, none of us are perfect in how we relate to others, but we must exercise discernment and remember that the devil wants us to believe the worst about others. Eventually, the pastor realized the truth, and life went on. However, this opened the young man's eyes to the fact that the Accuser is constantly at work.

The purpose of this story is not to demean or criticize anyone involved, but to illustrate how the devil can take any situation and even the best of intentions, and twist them for his purposes. This young man did not intend to offend anyone, but the Accuser of the brethren took advantage of the situation. This is why we must be vigilant. The Bible says: *"Be sober, be vigilant; because your adversary the devil, as a roaring* lion, walks about, seeking whom he may devour" (1 Peter 5:8). It took some time, but all parties involved eventually found healing from the effects of betrayal and accusation. No matter what the situation is, we must make a conscious decision to reject the lies of the Accuser and embrace the truth of God's Word.

The Story Behind Satan

We know the nature of Satan is accusation. But why? What is his motive for accusing God's people? Well, as we mentioned earlier, Satan was kicked out of heaven as a result of his rebellion. The Bible says:

> And there appeared another wonder in heaven; and behold a great red dragon, having seven heads and ten horns, and seven crowns upon his heads. And his tail drew the third part of the stars of heaven, and did cast them to the earth: and the dragon stood before the woman which was ready to be delivered, for to devour her child as soon as it was born.... And there was war in heaven: Michael and his angels fought against the dragon; and the dragon fought and his angels, and prevailed not; neither was their place found any more in heaven. And the great dragon was cast out, that old serpent, called the Devil, and Satan, which deceives the whole world: he was cast out into the earth, and his angels were cast out with him.
>
> (Revelation 12:3–4, 7–9)

This Scripture gives us great insight into the plight of the Accuser. He was lifted up in pride and desired to exalt himself above the Most High. (See Isaiah 14:14.) This rebellion sparked a war in the heavenly realm which the devil obviously lost. The verse that I would like to draw particular attention to, however, is this one: *"And his tail drew the third part of the stars of heaven, and did cast them to the earth."* What does this mean?

Well, in Scripture, the stars often represent celestial beings. In other words, the stars were angels. The devil was so persuasive in his grievance against God that he managed to convince one third of the angels to get on board with him. He spread his bitterness and offense to all who were willing to take heed to his accusations. Can you imagine being involved in the church split in heaven? That must have been something serious!

In the end, the heavenly host who sided with the devil lost their original estate in heaven. They were stripped of their influence and, ultimately, were cast down to the earth. Talk about the short end of the stick! Be careful whom you side with! Like the stars of the heaven, every time we give ear to slander, we run the risk of losing our influence and authority. Is vain chatter really worth the cost of your influence?

Satan's not in heaven anymore so he can't accuse God, but he can try to accuse us before God. He knows that man is God's most prized creation, filled with His power. Satan therefore delights in watching us stumble, in proving our unworthiness, in using us to trip one another up. He accuses us to God and to each other, and wants nothing more than for us to join in. You may have never considered the serious implications of accusation, but I charge you to reconsider.

Lessons from Job

One of the most provocative and controversial stories of the Bible is the story of Job. You may or may not be familiar it, but in a nutshell, the book of Job begins by describing him as a blameless man who feared God, lived an upright life, and stayed away from evil: *"There was a man in the land of Uz, whose name was Job; and that man was perfect and upright, and one that feared God, and eschewed evil"* (Job 1:1). On top of that, he was extremely rich! God was pleased with Job, and was "bragging" about him when Satan, the Accuser, told God that the only reason Job feared (that is, respected and honored) Him was because God had blessed him with so much. Satan argued that if God were to take away his home, his many possessions, his livelihood, and his family, Job would curse God to His face! That was bold.

Now what is Satan doing here? He is slandering Job! Remember, slander is making a false spoken statement that damages a person's reputation. Satan was basically saying that Job didn't really care about God, and that he was only doing what he thought he needed to do to keep the benefits and blessings rolling in! But God knew Job; He knew Job's heart, so He allowed Satan to throw all the evil he could at Job. He let Satan snatch away everything that Job had, yet Job never cursed God. In fact, in verse 20 of the first chapter, Job, having received the first few rounds of bad news in rapid succession including the horror that all of his children were dead, fell to the ground and *worshipped God* in his agony.

But Satan didn't give up. Being the liar that he is, he decided that Job only refrained from cursing God because in spite of everything, Job still had his health. If that were taken away, he would certainly curse God to His face. Wrong again! It got so bad that Job reached the point of crying out that he wished he had never been born, but he never turned away from God. To make matters worse, Job's religious friends went on a critical rampage, telling him why he was going through all these troubles, beginning with Eliphaz the Temanite who says, *"Remember, I pray you, who ever perished, being innocent? or where were the righteous cut off? Even as I have seen, they that plow iniquity, and sow wickedness, reap the same"* (Job 4:7–8). Sometimes people can be very helpful! They didn't realize that they were finishing the enemy's dirty work by adding more and more discouragement.

EVERY TIME WE PARTICIPATE IN GOSSIP OR SLANDER, WE ARE OPENING OUR LIVES TO AND ALIGNING OURSELVES WITH THE *"ACCUSER OF THE BRETHREN."*

In the end, God restored Job's health, gave him twice more than what he had before (double for his trouble!), and blessed him with more sons and daughters. There is much, much more to take away from what happened with Job, but one of the key things to learn from it is this: just because the Accuser hurls insults and slings accusations at and about you doesn't mean they're true. So don't allow yourself to be entangled with accusing and slandering others.

Do You Work for the Devil?

Some time ago, I asked a group I was teaching whether they worked for the devil. Of course they answered *no*! When we think of working for the devil, we think of some ominous ceremony with a bubbling cauldron in which a person sells their soul to Beelzebub. But I would like to contend that working for the devil is much subtler than that!

Maybe a better question would be: Who's agenda are you advancing: God's or the devil's? Every time we engage in or entertain slander, we are in fact working to advance the cause of the kingdom of darkness. In the moment we may feel justified or even entertained, but at what cost? Who is the beneficiary?

When you understand the nature of Satan, you will be able to discern whether something is of God or is of the devil. If we are honest, we can admit that there have been times we felt completely justified in our behavior when in fact it was contrary to the will and nature of God. Often people say to me, "But you don't understand! They hurt me!" Unfortunately, feeling hurt is no excuse to violate God's Word. Your feelings can deceive you if you are not careful. We must make a decision that God's Word will be the final authority in our lives, not our feelings.

I have personally seen the devastation that comes with following your feelings. Satan can manipulate your feelings! This doesn't mean that what you feel is always illegitimate, but you must make your feelings accountable to God's truth. The more we learn to subject our emotions to God's Word, the more freedom we will enjoy.

SATAN'S LIE:
IF YOU LOVE SOMEONE,
YOU CAN'T HURT THEM.
#ACCUSINGTHEACCUSER

One day while praying about my marriage, I found myself complaining to God about my wife. "If she only listened, and did this or that…." I went on and on telling God my grievances. The irony of this is that my wife is practically perfect. (I am the one with flaws!) Nonetheless, it didn't prevent me from complaining. All of a sudden, the Lord told me, "You sound like the devil! He is the Accuser of the brethren and accuses them before God, night and day. You are just sitting there accusing your wife!"

I was shocked! How could I sound like the devil? Because I had never considered the spirit in which I was coming to God. I am not alone in this folly. Countless believers operate in a spirit of accusation on a daily basis. Since this experience happened, I have never looked at this issue in the same way. Who would have thought that I was working against the plan of God by complaining about and accusing my wife?

We have a responsibility as believers to cover one another—not accuse one another. Once we get the revelation that we have been called by God to be ministers of reconciliation, it will change the way we approach our relationships with people and the way we deal with offenses.

SATAN'S LIE:
CHRISTIANS CAN'T WORK
FOR THE DEVIL.
#ACCUSINGTHEACCUSER

Who's the Boss?

Several years ago, there was a show on television called *Who's the Boss?* It was about a retired baseball player who worked as a live-in housekeeper for a divorced advertising executive and her son. The show explored the reversal of traditional male/female roles as the ex-baseball player stayed home to take care of the house, and the divorcée went off to work. I believe the title of this show represents a very important question that every believer must ask himself or herself: "Who's the boss?" In other words, to whom are you submitted?

The Bible says, *"Humble yourselves therefore under the mighty hand of God, that He may exalt you in due time"* (1 Peter 5:6). Earlier, we mentioned that many people put their feelings and emotions before the Word of God. There is nothing wrong with being aware of our feelings, but when they begin to eclipse our relationship with God, there is a serious problem. Too many Christians have adopted a practical philosophy that they are their own boss. The problem is, if you step into the role of "boss" you become responsible for every aspect of your own life and every situation you face.

Once someone falsely accused me at my workplace. It was a very serious accusation and it could have cost me my job. When I heard about it, I went into self-defense mode. I began to come up with arguments and counter-arguments against my accuser. I thought of ways I could fight the accusations and vindicate myself. I drafted a very articulate yet offensive email to the head of Human Resources. I was going to show them who's boss! Once I drafted this scholarly email, I hit the send button. Several minutes later, I got a visit from my manager, asking me to come to his office. All of a sudden, I began to question whether sending that email was a good idea.

As I walked into his office, I noticed that the head of HR was also in the room, sitting down near the desk. I knew that this was more than a casual discussion. In my mind, I had crafted the perfect defense, but by the time I was done speaking with my manager and the head of HR, I was embarrassed and a bit humiliated. You see *not guilty* is not the same as *innocent*. Though I was not guilty of everything I was being accused of, I had made some serious errors in the process.

As I was walking out of the manager's office, I heard God speak to me and say, "Stand still and see My salvation!" He told me that by attempting to fight my own battle, I was excluding Him from the situation. He reminded me that He was the boss and not me.

EVERY TIME WE ATTEMPT TO DEFEND OURSELVES FROM AN ACCUSATION, WE HINDER GOD FROM DEFENDING US.

The Bible says: *"The LORD is my light and my salvation; whom shall I fear? the LORD is the strength of my life; of whom shall I be afraid?"* (Psalm 27:1). So if God is our salvation, then why are we constantly attempting to save ourselves? If He is our defense, then why do we try so hard to defend ourselves? The Lord, through my manager and the head of HR, had told me to stand still. This went against everything that my natural instinct dictated to me, but I realized that I was not qualified for the job of being my own boss in this particular situation. As I reflected on the situation, I realized that there were many things that I did wrong, even though I felt I was the one falsely accused. God has a way of shining the flashlight back on us when we attempt to blame someone else. Finally, I relinquished my right to defend myself and I asked God to forgive me for walking in pride.

The person who accused me was eventually fired. I was not happy that they were terminated, but it taught me a very valuable lesson: God is in charge! He is the boss. If we would only follow His leading, we would experience a level of peace and wholeness that we can hardly fathom.

For Discussion

1. What are some ways that you've seen Christians unintentionally doing the devil's work?

2. Is it possible to feel something that is contrary to God's will? If so, give examples.

3. Have you ever been in a situation where you tried to be the boss but found peace in handing the reins over to God instead? Describe.

Practicum

1. Read Isaiah 14:12–21. Why do you think that Satan rebelled? Contrast with what Paul says about Jesus in Philippians 2:5–8.

2. Your meditation is your medication! Ponder what and who you have been giving ear to that may be altering your perspective and damaging your relationship with God and others. Consider: family, friends, acquaintances, radio shows, podcasts, TV shows, movies, blogs, social media, news media.

3. Are you working for the devil in your relationships? Go through the list slowly and ask the Spirit to prompt your heart if you have been acting as an accuser to any of the following. Consider: spouse, children, parents, siblings, church members, pastors, coworkers, neighbors, friends, local officials, national officials.

Testimony

I had just joined a great church, and everything seemed to be going well. But one day while I was serving in the church, my pastor happened to glance at me during the service. This look reminded me of a very traumatic experience I had had in a church years ago: I had been specifically and directly criticized from the pulpit. The negative emotions from that situation began to emerge. I thought to myself, "They don't want me here!" I immediately went into defensive mode and started to develop my exit plan.

However, instead of just running out the back door of the church, I tried to calm down and resolved to speak with the pastor. I later asked him why he didn't like me, and he was very confused. It turns out that he wasn't even looking at me at all—he was just scanning the room! I was so relieved. This experience showed me that I had some unresolved issues that I needed to work through. The pastors prayed with me and helped me to walk through these challenges. Now I am serving faithfully on the leadership team. None of this would have happened if I had just walked away.

—Barbara

Prayer

Father, in the name of Jesus, I thank You for the truth of Your Word. I know You love me with all of Your heart. I know that I am the apple of Your eye. I know that You are my Defender, and so as a result, I choose not to defend myself. Your name is a strong tower, and the righteous run into it and are saved. I recognize that every time I speak in defense of myself I hinder Your righteous judgment from coming forth; therefore, I will allow You to speak on my behalf. I take authority over the spirit of witchcraft, and I break its power off of any area of my life. I refuse to work for the devil in any shape, form, or fashion. I will resist him with every fiber of my being. I say no to the spirit of accusation, in the name of Jesus. I take responsibility for my thoughts and my actions. Father, I choose to be thankful for the things You've done in my life, and I refuse to complain, in the name of Jesus.

Amen!

3
THE POWER OF SLANDER

Death and life are in the power of the tongue: and they that love it
shall eat the fruit thereof.   (Proverbs 18:21)

Words are very powerful. The words we speak can either create or
destroy. They have the power of death or life! In fact, the words
that we speak give permission and access to good or evil. This principle
is most directly applicable to our relationship with other believers. Our
words are a vehicle of either blessing or cursing. Every word we speak can
hurt or heal.

You may think that I'm inclining a little toward exaggeration here—
does it really matter that much what we say? But if we look at the Bible,
we can find example after example of the power of the tongue. It is more
than a muscle that helps us to eat and taste—it is also a creative force.

In the beginning of creation, God *spoke* the world into existence. He
used the power of His Word to create the visible universe. In the same
manner, the first act of man in the garden of Eden was to name the an-
imals (an idiomatic expression denoting the attachment of identity and
purpose to people and things).

As we've seen, it was Eve's conversation with the Serpent that brought
death and sin into the world. The Serpent bewitched Eve by using his

words to manipulate and control her. Isn't it ironic that the very activity that God used as a vehicle to establish purpose and significance became the same vehicle that ushered in the curse?

This is still happening today! Have you ever listened to a person relay a story about someone else and by the time they were done speaking, you literally wanted to assault the person they were talking about? You, my friend, were a victim of slander. Yes, I said you were a *victim*! Why? Because the person who was being talked about was not the only one targeted by the enemy; the enemy also targeted *you*. He wanted to contaminate your heart and mind toward someone else. Be careful whom you allow to influence you. Be careful whom you allow to speak into your life!

Stay Out of Trouble

"Whoso keeps his mouth and his tongue keeps his soul from troubles" (Proverbs 21:23). The word *trouble* in this passage comes from the Hebrew word *tsarah*, which means distress, trouble, or vexation. Who would have thought that our tongue could be the source of much vexation in our own lives and in the lives of others? Yet this is exactly what the Word of God tells us. One of the first lessons that I learned as a believer was to not be so liberal with my mouth. The Bible says, *"In the multitude of words there wants not sin: but he that refrains his lips is wise"* (Proverbs 10:19).

This isn't so different from the lesson that many of us learned as children. I can remember many an occasion where two or three kids were fighting, something broke or somebody got hurt, and then everybody had a story to tell the grown-ups. "He threw this! She said that! He punched me and I rolled into the lamp!" And you know what the grown-ups would say? *"I don't need to know everything!"* Just so, we as Christians don't need to know everything, either. Pastors don't need to know everything. Leaders don't need to know everything. Members don't need to know everything.

Many Christians suffer from what I call "Foot in Mouth Disease." I will never forget one time I was talking about someone to another person, and the person said to me, "Stop saying those things! That's my sister!" Now, I shouldn't have been saying those things in the first place! But I learned that day that I needed to use care when speaking about others, because you never know who or what you are affecting by the words you speak.

The Tale of Two Tongues

Where does slander start? Inside our mouths. The apostle James uses a bunch of helpful metaphors to help us understand the power of the words spoken by our tongues:

Behold also the ships, which though they be so great, and are driven of fierce winds, yet are they turned about with a very small helm, wherever the governor lists. Even so the tongue is a little member, and boasts great things. Behold, how great a matter a little fire kindles! And the tongue is a fire, a world of iniquity: so is the tongue among our members, that it defiles the whole body, and sets on fire the course of nature; and it is set on fire of hell. For every kind of beasts, and of birds, and of serpents, and of things in the sea, is tamed, and has been tamed of mankind: but the tongue can no man tame; it is an unruly evil, full of deadly poison. Therewith bless we God, even the Father; and therewith curse we men, which are made after the similitude of God. Out of the same mouth proceeds blessing and cursing. My brethren, these things ought not so to be. Does a fountain send forth at the same place sweet water and bitter? Can the fig tree, my brethren, bear olive berries? either a vine, figs? so can no fountain both yield salt water and fresh. (James 3:4–12)

The Bible says that our tongue can be an unruly evil. It is a fountain out of which flows both sweet and bitter water. This is the paradox of the Christian life: with one mouth we bless God and with the same mouth we curse men.

The apostle John later says, "*If a man say, I love God, and hates his brother, he is a liar*" (1 John 4:20). You may say to me, "What does that have to do with it? I do not hate my brother!" But we must define what hatred really means. And before we can define hatred, we must define love. Love speaks no ill toward its neighbor. Instead, when we love someone we cover them; we bless them. The inverse is true of hatred. When we hate someone, we speak evil of that person. It can be as simple as being slightly envious of someone's continued success and sending up a wish that they would fail. Or hoping that someone will be exposed. But this is not the love of God! The Bible says that love covers a multitude of sins. (See 1 Peter 4:8.) The Bible says, whoever keeps his mouth and tongue keeps his soul from troubles. (See Proverbs 21:23.)

Many years ago I was involved in a conversation about a particular pastor in our area. This pastor had a very questionable reputation and had found himself in the middle of scandalous allegations. Because the church was large and important, everyone knew about this pastor and his circumstances. He was also very wealthy, and many people criticized him for his opulent lifestyle. While speaking with some men in our church, I began to join in with them as they criticized this pastor. We were even laughing about some aspects of his life.

SATAN'S LIE: IT'S NOT SLANDER IF IT'S ABOUT SOMEBODY FAMOUS.
#POWEROFSLANDER

But while I was standing there, I heard a still small voice speak to me, saying, *They will talk about you the same way.* I immediately became quiet. I thought to myself, *How could they ever speak of me in that manner?* What I did not understand is that circumstances are temporary and things are always subject to change. Who would've thought that just a few years later I would have a growing, thriving church in the same area? Who would've thought that I would find myself susceptible to identical accusations? After all, I wasn't even a pastor back then!

Whether this pastor had done much wrong or not, the moral of the story remains: Be careful what you say. Be careful whom you make fun of. Be careful whom you speak against. Because whatever you sow, you will reap. As we saw earlier, the Bible tells us very plainly that life and death are in the power of the tongue and they that love it will eat its fruit. This suggests to us that our words are seeds. Every seed has the capacity to produce a harvest. The pastor that they spoke evil about is still preaching and teaching the Word of God. I have learned that man's period is often God's comma!

Once we understand the significance of the words we speak, it will change the way that we approach relationships both inside and outside the church.

The Double-Edged Sword

The Bible says that the Word of God is like a weapon:

For the word of God is quick, and powerful, and sharper than any two-edged sword, piercing even to the dividing asunder of soul and spirit, and of the joints and marrow, and is a discerner of the thoughts and intents of the heart. (Hebrews 4:12)

God's Word spoken from His mouth is a sword. This double-edged sword is unique because it has the ability to pierce and to discern, to cut and to heal, to correct and to conceal. It often reminds me of the surgical instrument of a master surgeon. He has the ability to take the same knife that someone could use to murder a victim and use it instead to perform a life-giving heart transplant.

Did you realize that your words have a similar power? They can be used to hurt or to heal. Jesus said that by your words you will be justified and by your words you will be condemned. (See Matthew 12:37.) That's why it's so important to be careful with our words.

I know firsthand the tragedy of speaking words without consideration. When I was growing up as a young believer, I was very judgmental. I would often ask myself, *Why don't people just get it? Why did this brother make that mistake? Why did that sister make such a bad decision?* I just did not understand! If they were only as spiritual as I was they wouldn't have these problems—right? Little did I know that I would have my share of struggles in the future.

You see, the mercy you extend toward others is the same mercy that will be extended toward you. The Bible puts it this way, *"With the merciful You will show Yourself merciful; with an upright man You will show Yourself upright"* (Psalm 18:25). The reality is, everything we speak directly impacts our lives. I was judgmental and impatient with others because I had yet to come to terms with the reality of my own condition. I was in desperate need of grace and mercy myself. When you show mercy to others, God extends mercy to you in your darkest hour. However, if you show intolerance and criticism toward others, you will ultimately receive the same.

Many years ago there was a famous televangelist who had a serious and very public moral failure. Due to the wide reach of his television ministry, everyone witnessed his humiliating scandal. In fact, one of the most vocal and instrumental individuals during this time was another popular televangelist. He even helped to expose the scandal. However, later, this same man who was so eager to expose another was caught in scandal himself. How ironic! He violated the biblical law of "Judge not, lest you be judged." (See Matthew 7:1.) He suffered the same (if not more) shame, embarrassment, and humiliation as his fallen brother. Why? I call it the insanity of hypocrisy! In the book of Romans, it says: *Therefore you are inexcusable, O man, whosoever you are that judges: for wherein you judge another, you condemn yourself; for you that judge do the same things* (Romans 2:1). Today, by the grace of God, both of these ministers have been restored. However, the point remains—slander is never a blessing!

SATAN'S LIE: IF IT'S ANONYMOUS, IT'S NO BIG DEAL.
#POWEROFSLANDER

Whenever we judge others (specifically by speaking against them), we end up condemning ourselves. If only we could learn this very valuable lesson! What if I told you that every time you spoke a negative word about someone a dagger literally penetrated their body? Would you speak evil about them? (I hope it doesn't depend on the situation!) Many of us would be guilty of murder by the time the day was over.

The reason why we don't look at things in this way is because we often surrender our ideals to a culture that exonerates us from responsibility of the words we speak. We believe that we can say whatever we want and there will be no retribution.

Unfortunately, the proliferation of social media has exacerbated this problem. The computer screen and keyboard have apparently given people license to say whatever they want. There is a term for this phenomena—trolling! Just like the mythical troll laid wait under the bridge for innocent travelers to cross over before attacking, the social media troll hides under the bridge of anonymity and attacks people simply because they crossed its path, and without any regard for the damaging nature of the things they type. We mustn't be trolls, beloved: God has called us to be lambs—gentle and obedient to the Good Shepherd, who leads us in the paths of righteousness for His name's sake.

Speak Life!

This is why we must be careful in what we say about other people. The Bible says to *"speak not evil of one another, brethren"* (James 4:11). Let me ask you a question. What was the name of the person who committed sexual sin in the Corinthian church? The reason you cannot possibly answer this question is because Paul never mentioned his name. It was never printed in the bulletin or published in any magazine or tabloid. While it is true that Paul corrected a sin, he did not do so at the expense of the reputation and well-being of his fallen brother. The problem is that people don't know the difference between "exposing people" and exposing the enemy. We often mistake "correcting" someone with shaming that person. These are two mutually exclusive concepts. To correct means to identify a wrong behavior or action and bring truth and instruction so that the person can change their behavior. This is totally different from writing a demeaning article about someone who made a mistake or from speaking negatively about someone's struggle or failure. What could the struggling person possibly benefit from by such actions?

EVERYTHING ABOUT THE ACCUSER IS TO EXPOSE, INDICT, AND CONDEMN, WHILE EVERYTHING ABOUT THE HOLY SPIRIT IS TO CONVICT, CORRECT, AND HEAL.

One day, I was reading an article in a Christian magazine. This article was discussing the moral failure of a particular pastor. But I noticed that there was no encouragement, reconciliation, or restoration in the tone of the article. It was almost like the author was relishing the pastor's moral failure and was hoping for a negative outcome. I am not attempting to presume the intent of the writer of this article, but the pervasive tone that came across to the reader was condemnation, condemnation, condemnation.

As I continued to read the article, my spirit became grieved. I knew that the Spirit of God was not glorified in this. In fact it was saturated with the clandestine nature of the Accuser. Everything about the Accuser (aka Satan) is to expose, indict, and condemn, while everything about the Holy Spirit is to convict, correct, and heal.

How could a Christian article report and promote such negativity in the name of the Lord? Don't they realize that this is not beneficial to anyone? Quite simply, they probably didn't recognize the power and negative impact of their words. Like I said before, every time we speak about someone or to someone, our words have a tangible effect. I have heard many people say that it is our responsibility to expose people when they fall or fail. They say that we must "expose the enemy." I agree with the latter statement. The first statement is absolutely false and anti-biblical.

SATAN'S LIE: IT'S OUR JOB TO EXPOSE EVERYBODY ELSE.
#POWEROFSLANDER

Jesus modeled a totally different lifestyle. In the story of the woman caught in adultery, Jesus does the unthinkable. While the religious leaders were ready to accuse, condemn, and ultimately kill this woman for her sin, Jesus issued a profound command: let he that is without sin cast the first stone. (See John 8:7.) The Bible tells us that those men dropped the stones and went their way. Jesus then looked at the embarrassed woman and asked, "Where are your accusers?" She responded that they had left. Then Jesus said the most beautiful, life-giving words: *"Neither do I condemn you: go, and sin no more"* (John 8:11). In this profound biblical instance, Jesus spoke life to a dead situation.

When was the last time that we considered our responsibility to speak life to a person or situation that seems dead or defeated? I want you to imagine that your son or your daughter had a very debilitating failure in their life. Would you write to the most popular tabloid in your city? Would you call the news media and give them the juicy gossip? No! You would discipline your son or daughter privately, and you would speak life to him or her in order to restore them. Such is the path laid out for us in the book of James:

> *Brethren, if any of you do err from the truth, and one convert him; let him know, that he which converts the sinner from the error of his way shall save a soul from death, and shall hide a multitude of sins.*
> (James 5:19–20)

The apostle James admonished the church to bring truth to error in such a way that causes the one in error to be converted. The Greek word *epistrephō* used here means, "to return back, or to return to love." This is a very powerful truth. Every person in the body of Christ has a responsibility to call each other back to the truth.

However, then James says something very interesting: "*He which converts the sinner from the error of his way shall save a soul from death, and shall hide a multitude of sins.*" The word *hide* here is the Greek word *kalyptō*, which means: to hide, veil, or hinder the knowledge of a thing. Contrary to popular opinion, God is often in the business of covering sin, not exposing it! This is not a matter of lying, deceiving, or manipulating. Rather, just as a parent covers their children, God covers us from being exposed. Once a person turns from their error, the grace of God covers and conceals their sin and brings them to a place of restoration.

However, if we are always attempting to uncover people's faults by speaking evil against them, we are unwittingly working against the plan of God. I want you to consider yourself for a moment. How many things has God concealed about you? How many things have you said and done privately that God never exposed publicly? How, then, can you (or I!) have the audacity to operate in self-righteousness and pride and parade ourselves as judge, jury, and executioner? You might want to think twice before being so quick to speak.

The Tongue of the Learned

In my many years of ministry, I have realized that people need to be encouraged, uplifted, and strengthened. The Accuser seeks to discourage, abuse, and weaken the bride of Christ, but God is about to unmask his evil schemes and set us free once and for all! Isaiah the prophet gave a powerful prophecy:

The Lord God has given me the tongue of the learned, that I should know how to speak a word in season to him that is weary: He wakens morning by morning, He wakens my ear to hear as the learned.

(Isaiah 50:4)

Every time I minister, I ask the Lord to give me the *"tongue of the learned."* I ask Him to teach me how to speak a word in season to those who may be weary. One of the easiest ways to develop the tongue of the learned is to listen to the voice of God. Every morning when we arise, we must ask God to speak to us and show us His perfect will for our lives.

We must also ask God to give us His heart for people. One of the reasons we are often so quick to speak a word of death is because we don't see people the way God sees them. The truth is we may not even see *ourselves* the way God sees us—so how can we see others in the right light?

A dear pastor friend of mine told me a story that shook me to my core. He told me that there was a pastor in his city that had a moral failure. This pastor was fairly popular and had a growing church, but when the news of his failing was made public, he lost everything—including his family. No one would associate with this pastor anymore and the church disintegrated. Several years later, my friend ran into this pastor at a restaurant. As he glanced at him, he heard the Holy Spirit say, "Go speak to him and love on him." So he went over to the table and said, "Bishop, how are you? I love you, sir!" He gave him a hug and encouraged him. Tears welled up in the pastor's eyes. As my friend walked away, the Lord said, "You could be sitting where he is and he could be sitting where you are!" The pastor who told me this story was so humbled by this experience that it left an indelible mark on his heart, just as it did on mine. This is why we must refuse to be brokers of death. Instead, we must speak life!

May the Lord grant us the wisdom and the grace to use our words for His purposes. (See Ephesians 4:29.) Let's ensure that we are edifying our brothers and sisters in Christ rather than tearing them down. Before you speak something about another person, take a moment to consider the profound impact of your words.

For Discussion

1. Why do you think God judges us according to our words? (See Matthew 12:33–37.)

2. What's our responsibility when we see a sister or a brother straying from the truth?

3. Was there a time when someone spoke life to you instead of death? Describe.

Testimony

One of my members, whom I helped and poured into for years, became offended with me over something I did. Instead of coming to me and seeking clarity and understanding, they left the church in haste and frustration. Then they went to other members in the church and slandered me. This was very painful. To make matters worse, they began to tell lies about me even to those closest to me. I was so angry that I wanted them to pay for their actions. One day, the Holy Spirit began to convict my heart, and let me know that He was in control. He showed me areas of immaturity and sin in my own heart. I repented before the Lord and blessed this person from the bottom of my heart. Though the relationship did not go back to its original state, I was able to find peace and freedom as I released every offense. —*Emeka*

Prayer

Father, Your Word declares that life and death are in the power of the tongue. I recognize that my tongue has the power to bring life or death. As of this moment, I choose to speak life over every situation and person that I come into contact with. Show me Your love for others, so that I may love them that way, too. Before I speak about another person, I will consider the profound impact of my words. I choose to speak blessing and healing over my brothers and sisters in Christ. May my words be a vehicle to save lives and turn others from the error of their ways! Give me the tongue of the learned that I may speak a word in season to him or her that may be weary. Awaken my ears to hear as the learned, in the name of Jesus.

Amen!

4

SAY NO TO GOSSIP

*He that goes about as a **talebearer** reveals secrets: therefore meddle not with him that flatters with his lips.* (Proverbs 20:19)

In the early 90s, there was a show on television called *In Living Color*. It was essentially a comedy show, where each of the comedians would re-enact "situation comedy" skits. One featured a woman named Miss Bonita. This unemployed, middle-aged, African-American woman would hang out of her urban apartment window in New York and spend her days talking to the neighbors from her window and then addressing the audience. Her favorite adage was, "I ain't one to gossip but...," and of course, she would go on to disclose the secrets of each person passing by.

On the show, it was hilarious. But in real life, it's not as funny. And this very Miss-Bonita-like act goes on in far too many of our churches. Scores of believers do not realize the damaging effect of the gossip they engage in. Countless others use it as a plausible outlet to express their boredom and their frustrations. Like Miss Bonita, they poke their heads in everyone else's business and look for ways to enjoy the next exciting tidbit of information about people inside and outside the church.

Whether you realize it or not, gossip is strictly prohibited in Scripture. Make no mistakes—it is a sin! God commanded the Israelites saying, *"You shall not go up and down as a talebearer among your people"* (Leviticus 19:16). In the book of Proverbs, the Bible says that a talebearer's words are like wounds. (See Proverbs 26:22.)

When was the last time you considered that gossip can wound deeply?

The Effect of Gossip

There was a lady I knew many years ago who reminded me of Miss Bonita. She had the scoop on every person you can think of. She told me about every minister in town, every secret thing that anyone had ever done, and every kind of car or house that everyone owned. When scandal broke out, she was the first person to know about it.

Then one day, scandal came to visit her at her front door. Her own people were involved in some deeply disturbing activities. It took that extreme situation for her to realize people will have to reap what they have sown. She thought that what she was doing wasn't all that bad—because it had never affected her. But once she and her family were at risk, she quickly changed her opinion. Though this was a very painful experience for her, she learned to be compassionate to others through her own brokenness. The good news is that her family recovered from the devastation and life moved on.

So what really constitutes as gossip? I define it as casual or unconstrained conversation and reports about other people, typically involving details that were intended to be private or are not confirmed as being true.

Ok, now let me give you a definition of the *effect* of gossip. When my daughters were younger we would put beads in their hair. These beads came in different colors and hues, but they were all the same size. Every now and then, our daughter's beads would come loose and they would spill all over the floor. Sometimes there would be twenty, sometimes there would be thirty or more beads on the floor. No big deal! All we have to do is pick him up off the floor. Right? The problem is that when you get down on your hands and knees, you can't hardly find them all! Those beads would bounce and scatter all over our living room and our entire kitchen. Sometimes you'd find beads in the strangest places that had fallen three months ago!

Gossip works the same way. Once you release it, it goes further and wider than you could ever imagine or have ever intended, and it's nearly impossible to retrieve. Once it has been spoken, it can't be called back.

Many years ago, I watched a movie called *Doubt* about a Catholic priest who was under suspicion of having an inappropriate relationship with one of the young boys in the church. I don't mean to go into detail about the movie, but it had one story that I'll never forget.

There was a woman who came to the parish priest for confession and told him that she had a problem with gossiping. She said that she couldn't control herself. Every time new information came across her ears she would spread it without validating or verifying the information. She asked the priest what she should do to overcome this vice. He told her to go home, get a pillow, climb onto a roof, cut the pillow open, and then to come back. So the woman left and did exactly what he said. Then she came back to the priest. "Did you cut open the pillow?" he asked. "Yes," she replied. "What happened?" he asked. She explained how once she stabbed the pillow, feathers came out and flew everywhere, all around her and all over town. The priest told her to then go gather all the feathers. "That's impossible!" she said.

"And that," the priest replied, "is what gossip does."

I learned a very valuable lesson from this story. Once you say something about someone else to another person, it is impossible to take it back. This is what makes gossip so very, very dangerous.

Toxicity of Gossip

As young kids growing up in Atlanta, I and my friends often played outside in the yard all day long. Something I will never forget is the smell of the septic tank on the side of our house. Anytime it would run over, there would be a foul odor that permeated the whole yard. They say that our sense of smell is the strongest sense attached to memories, and it must be true because I can remember this smell like it was yesterday. The smell of sewage is very hard to forget.

This septic tank has no stronger a stench than gossip in the church. Quite frankly, gossip is akin to toxic waste: it is foul, poisonous, and disgusting. Many Christians have become septic in their thoughts, attitudes, and relationships. In other words, they are infected with hurt and bitterness and they are "overflowing" into the lives of others. Every person they meet and speak with inevitably becomes contaminated by the pain and hurt that they carry.

If I asked you to eat the drainage from a septic tank, I am sure you would be appalled by my request, yet how many times have you sat and entertained gossip? Remember, the one who hears gossip is just as guilty as the one who spreads it! And if they will talk about someone else to your face, they will talk to someone else about you behind your back!

Are you familiar with the term "Agent Orange"? It's a chemical mixture that was used by the US military during the Vietnam War. They sprayed it over vast acres to kill forest cover and make easier targets out of North Vietnamese and Viet Cong troops. It was also used to destroy crops that could sustain the enemy troops. This powerful chemical not only stripped plants and trees of their leaves and life, it also, as was later discovered, had the long-term effects of tumors, birth defects, rashes, psychological illness, and cancer. The Vietnamese population and US servicemen and their families were devastated by these unexpected and disastrous effects. Talk about a "quick fix" gone wrong! What was meant to only kill plants ended up killing people.

Can you see how this can be compared to gossip? Too often, we assume the outcome of the words we "spray" will be what we plan and nothing more, and that there won't be any long term effects. We brush it off our consciences with phrases like, "I was just saying." We couldn't be more wrong! Every time we speak, we are never "just saying" anything, but we are always sowing seeds. And remember, seeds sown produce harvests. Gossiping about our brothers and sisters exposes and makes targets out of them, whether you realized it before the deed or not. Gossip spreads like a sickness, and can easily kill someone's character. This is why God prohibits it.

The Bible says, "*A good man out of the good treasure of his heart brings forth that which is good; and an evil man out of the evil treasure of his heart brings forth that which is evil: for of the abundance of the heart his mouth speaks*" (Luke 6:45). I believe that many Christians need to go through a soul detox. They must be sanitized in their mind and heart. How do we experience this cleansing? First, we must meditate in the Word of God and reestablish our thought life on the foundation of God's truth.

Second, we must abstain from any and all forms of gossip and offense. Just as a drug addict has to go through a physiological detox, so must the offended person detoxify themselves from any and all offense.

Gossip Distorts Truth

We live in an interesting era, often referred to as the information age. People have more access to information than they've ever had at any point in history. As a result of this, news, gossip, scandal, and other deplorable information is only one click of a button away. This phenomenon has deeply affected our culture and has greatly influenced the church.

SATAN'S LIE:
TALKING ABOUT FRIENDS
IS NO DIFFERENT FROM
SCROLLING THROUGH FACEBOOK.
#SAYNOTOGOSSIP

When I was a kid, I used to play a game called "telephone" with my friends. Everybody sat down in a row, and the first person would come up with a sentence like "the cat got sick yesterday" and would whisper it in the ear of the next person. Without clarifying what they heard, the second kid would whisper the sentence into the ear of the third kid, and so on all the way down the line. By the end, the sentence was usually a bunch of gobbledygook!

In the same way, gossip twists the truth. Whatever you hear through gossip is always a distortion of the facts. Have you ever developed strong negative emotions about a person that you never had any interaction or conversation with? Why? It's usually because someone told you something about another person and you took his or her word as gospel rather than investigating it for yourself. Now, it is certainly appropriate to ask for opinions or advice, especially when our safety is at stake. But when, in social situations, we use gossip as our main source of information, we are walking in great error.

Have you ever tried to defend someone when you didn't even know all the details of what they did? My pastor told me about one time when he did. He was counselling a woman who was having problems with her husband. She started telling the pastor about all the things her husband was doing: being verbally abusive, emotionally abusive, and mentally abusive toward her, playing mind games. My pastor said that he became so angry in the counselling session, he wanted to go find the husband immediately and confront him. He said as much to the woman, but the Lord interrupted him and said, "Son? Ask her how she got him." My pastor said to the woman, "I don't know why the Lord is telling me this, but He told me to ask you how you met this man." The woman hung her head. It turned out that she took him from his last wife. The husband became bitter when he realized the woman who stole him wasn't all that much different from the woman he was stolen from. The Lord gave my pastor the wisdom to walk this woman through the pain and heal her marriage, but it was a process.

My point after this story is simple: before you jump, before you make a decision, before you take a side, before you act, you need to know what's actually going on in the situation. And you can't know that if your mind has become distorted by the words of another. I have a policy in my life: I do not defend any situation until I know to the best of my ability the character and the actions of all involved.

One of the worst forms of gossip is the kind that we spiritualize. This is so prevalent in the church. Some people even have the audacity to refer to this as *discernment*. Biblical discernment is not even in the same category as gossip! One originates from the Holy Spirit; the other one originates from the flesh. I would take it one step further—the other originates in the pit of hell.

Please don't misunderstand me; I believe the gifts of the Spirit, including discernment of spirits, are very important. However, I also believe that the gifts of the Spirit come with a mantle of responsibility. If God shows you something about someone else, you have the biblical responsibility to pray for that person, not gossip about him or her.

My favorite version of spiritualized gossip is whatever comes in the form of, "We need to pray about...." This phrase has been used to cover up more gossip and slander than there are seats at the Super Bowl. Religious people use this method to disarm their listeners—and to deceive themselves about the morality of bringing it up. "We need to pray about so-and-so's addiction." "We need to pray about so-and-so, their kids aren't coming to church anymore." "We need to pray for so-and-so, they are having a terrible year and aren't responding well."

SATAN'S LIE: GOSSIP ONLY TEMPTS OLDER WOMEN.
#SAYNOTOGOSSIP

I was talking to some colleagues one day and they shared a conversation that they had with one of their friends. They were trying to convince their friend that her pastor was just wrong about something in particular. And now they were telling me the whole situation in the hopes that I would back up their accusation of this pastor! I asked them one question: how would they feel if it was *their* pastor being talked about in this way? They were silent.

The problem with gossip is that it often dehumanizes and devalues its victims. If you are ever sharing a little tidbit about someone and wonder, *Is this gossip?* I have a rule of thumb for you. Ask yourself, *Would I want someone to say this about me?* If not, then for heaven's sake, don't say it! Another is to ask yourself, *Would I say this if the brother/sister I'm talking about were right here in the room?* If the answer is no, then for heaven's sake, don't say it!

Let me be clear; God hates gossip! Why is this so difficult to understand? Why do we believe that it's a minor offense to tear down our brother or sister in Christ? Solomon wrote, "*a whisperer separates chief friends*" (Proverbs 16:28), and Paul ranks gossip with quarreling, jealousy, and conceit as sins that he hopes not to find in the church: "*For I fear that perhaps when I come I may find you not as I wish, and that you may find me not as you wish—that perhaps there may be quarreling, jealousy, anger, hostility, slander, gossip, conceit, and disorder*" (2 Corinthians 12:20 ESV).

We must hold ourselves responsible for the gossip that we speak! In the early 1960s, a Yale psychologist conducted a series of social experiments that shocked the world. The diverse study participants were placed in a room in front of a box with a lever that administered electric shocks in levels of intensity from one to ten. Through the glass the participant could see the adjacent room where an actor, the "learner," was hooked up to the box. The participant, however, had no idea that it was an actor; they thought it was another participant. The participant would be instructed to administer shocks to the learner for each wrong answer. A third person, the experimenter, would read the questions and instruct the participant on when to administer the shocks. Most participants showed trepidation in the initial stages, but after the experimenter assured them that they would be exempt from any responsibility, they reluctantly obliged. As they administered the shock, that actor would scream in pain. After certain duration, the participant would be told to raise the lever to level 10, which was deadly. They were again reassured that all responsibility rested on the experimenter, and in the majority of cases, the participant would comply!

This study demonstrates the terrible things we are capable of when we think we're not responsible. The reason why many Christians engage in gossip is that they mistakenly believe they are exempt from responsibility to the parties involved. Nothing could be further from the truth. What if I told you that every time you gossiped, someone died? Would you still engage in it? The spiritual damage of gossip can be far worse than any physical death.

Spiritual Cannibalism

In nature, there are only a few species that eat their own kind. This phenomenon is considered an anomaly. In the world of humans, those who engage in this practice are considered cannibals—and it's one of the most infamous abominations.

Yet there is another species that has a tendency to devour their own kind: Christians! Paul warns the church, *"But if you bite and devour one another, take heed that you be not consumed one of another"* (Galatians 5:15). The Judaizers were engaging in spiritual cannibalism. Many saints today are guilty of the same thing. Every time you gossip, backbite, criticize or slander a brother or sister in Christ, you are "devouring" them. Yes, they may be in one piece physically, but their reputation and esteem have been cannibalized.

The consequences of actual cannibalism are severe. Research on a tribe that traditionally practiced funerary cannibalism demonstrated that their cannibalism resulted in an incurable degenerative neurological disorder.[1] The same is true of spiritual cannibalism. When we devour our own kind through slander and gossip, we become sick and shorten the life spans of our own destiny.

Sometimes, this cannibalism is subtle. Have you ever talked with someone who "cast a shadow" over another person with their words? When you mention the name of the individual, they make a face or express disdain for the person non-verbally. This is the same as speaking evil of another. Don't be a spiritual cannibal! Don't judge and gossip about your brothers or sisters in Christ. Bless and curse not! Do good to them that despitefully use you and persecute you. Remember, you are what you eat!

As the days grow darker and darker, the church must unite and walk in love like never before. The spirits of slander and gossip have been proliferating in the body of Christ, but it is time for us to make a change. It is time for the church to resist the temptation to throw our brothers and sisters under the bus. It is time to stop devouring one another and instead walk in forgiveness and compassion toward each other. I believe that Christ is returning to a glorious, loving bride, not a church of wolves and cannibals.

For Discussion

1. Have you ever been gossiped about? What was your response?

2. Why does gossip never seem to keep the facts straight?

3. Is it too strong to call gossip "spiritual cannibalizing"? Why or why not?

Practicum

1. Social media has made it easier to speak death—but also to speak life! Make a point this month of changing the majority of your

---

1. "Fore," Encyclopedia of World Cultures, Encyclopedia.com, http://www. encyclopedia.com/humanities/encyclopedias-almanacs-transcripts-and-maps/fore (November 9, 2016).

posts from negative to positive, and notice what kind of response you get.

2. Take time to detoxify from gossip. Make it a prayer topic in your quiet time for a week. Ask that God would open your eyes to where you gossip whether you notice it or not. Command the devil to stop tempting you with gossip and meditate on Ephesians 4:29; Colossians 4:6; Proverbs 15:7; 1 Thessalonians 5:11; Proverbs 25:11–12; and Proverbs 15:2–4.

3. Using the questions, "Would I want this said about me?" and "Would I say this if the topic of conversation were here in the room?" keep a tally over the period of a week of how many comments you hold back. Are you surprised?

Testimony

At one point in my life, I was having arguments with my spouse more and more often. It was as if the enemy was whispering accusations in my ear about them. The more I listened to these accusations, the angrier I became. At some point, I had to ask myself, "Why am I angry?" The more I began to examine myself, the more I realized that this anger did not come from me directly, but was instigated by the enemy. These were insecurities that I felt within myself that I in turned projected onto my spouse. Dr. Kynan taught us that Satan is the Accuser of the brethren, and that many times Satan speaks in the first person. I began to fall out of agreement with those ungodly thoughts and all of a sudden the anger and the frustration began to break. I was able to humble myself and go to my spouse and seek forgiveness, healing, and restoration. Now I know to watch out for the Accuser trying to whisper to my mind.   —*Anonymous*

Prayer

Father, in the name of Jesus, I thank You for who You are and all that You have done in my life. Today I recognize the destructive nature of gossip. I recognize that gossip is an abomination and that it does not glorify Your name. I ask You to forgive me for participating in gossip in any shape, form, or fashion, whether I was speaking or listening. I recognize that every person in the body of Christ is my brother or sister; therefore, I choose not to hear any words that do not edify the body of Christ. Lord, may I only speak those words that please You. I ask these things in the name of Jesus.

Amen!

5
THE SPIRIT OF OFFENSE

Late one Saturday night, as I sat in my bed, something came over me. Lights suddenly began flashing all around me and I found myself moving through time and space. Was this a vision? Was this a dream? I do not know, but I do know that in a matter of seconds I was standing at the very scene of the crucifixion. As the dust filled the air, I heard the groaning of our Lord while He agonized on the cross. The cracking of whips pierced my ears. I could see the Roman soldiers. I could see the crowd. I could even see the phylacteries of the Pharisees who stood by, watching the most heinous crime in history unfold. What was happening? As my gaze was transfixed on the face of the Savior of the world, I heard a voice speak: "My son, I took all of the offenses of the world so that you would no longer have to live in offense."

In moments, I was back to myself. This vision (or dream) resonated in my heart. I realized that offense is a *spiritual* issue, and that it that has plagued the church for far too long. It should disappear the moment we realize what Christ accomplished on the cross—but it doesn't.

How many people reading this book have been saved for longer than a day? OK, if you've been saved longer than twenty-four hours, you know beyond a shadow of a doubt that offenses are a real part of being a believer. If you have attended any church service anywhere in the world, you have probably discovered that there are an endless number of things and people that have the potential to be offensive: the manner and tone in which a brother, sister, church administrator, or elder speaks to us; whether or not we are acknowledged by somebody; when a particular office or duty is withheld from us…the scenarios are endless. A man once told me the way we mounted our televisions on the wall in the church were unbearable to him. Talk about an obsession!

We can all point to experiences that were somehow offensive. But although we may know it intuitively, what does it actually mean to be offended? Where does it come from? How do we know when we are offended? And more importantly, how do we break free from a spirit of offense?

Once you discover the answers to these important questions you will learn to recognize the enemy's schemes before they ever materialize. Let's get started.

Offenses Will Come

I spent a huge number of hours in church when I was a kid. In fact, sometimes my mother would take me to church against my will! This was just the life that we lived, especially growing up in the South. As one who has never been a stranger to the church environment, I am also no stranger to offense. Quite frankly, offense and I have gotten to know each other very well over the years. Jesus told the disciples,

> *It is impossible but that offenses will come.... Take heed to yourselves: If your brother trespass against you, rebuke him; and if he repent, forgive him. And if he trespass against you seven times in a day, and seven times in a day turn again to you, saying, I repent; you shall forgive him.* (Luke 17:1, 3–4)

Let's think about that first part again: *"It is impossible but that offenses will come."* In other words, it's not possible for us not to experience offense! Do you know why? Because Satan wants us offended! He wants us discouraged! He wants the church community to be distrustful; he wants the church to be distracted so it will not come together to fulfill its purpose. We have to serve the devil notice that offense will not hinder us today! We are un-offendable, in Jesus' name!

Beyond the fact that the devil wants us to be offended, we must also understand that people are fundamentally flawed (apart from Christ). And where there are flawed people, there will always be the propensity for offense.

But Jesus went further to say that if your brother trespasses against you, forgive him. What does the term *trespass* mean? When you think of trespassing, think of a property that says "No Trespassing" on it. It means that you can't step on that property, you can't go past that sign. Jesus was specifically dealing with the offenses in a relational context: those specific areas in our lives where people stepped past a boundary that we had established in our heart or in our mind. The person went into territory that they should not have been in. They stepped into areas that were off-limits.

Now the problem with relational trespassing is that most people don't know which areas are off-limits—for their friends or even for themselves! Boundaries are often based on experiences that we have had in the past, are different for each person, and can be unpredictable. For example, if a church member has experienced harsh words and verbal abuse from a church leader in the past, they—perhaps without even realizing it—will have a low tolerance for any church leaders. They are being tormented by ghosts from the past.

The Haunted House

What is it about haunted houses that hold such attraction for kids? I remember going to school during the season of Halloween and my classmates would be full of horrific stories of their experiences in haunted houses. Old buildings would be converted into terrifying mazes with ghouls that jumped out at you, ghost sounds over the loudspeaker, and every manner of creative ways to scare.

Well, I don't believe in ghosts, but I do believe that many believers are living inside a haunted house. What do I mean by this? Many Christians are being haunted and even tormented in their minds by negative experiences. They are constantly reminded of their hurt and disappointment. These "ghosts" inhabit the house of their mind, will, and emotions.

When bad things happen to us, the mind paints a picture of them and attaches it to specific feelings and emotions. This is why certain people and places remind us strongly of previous experiences. Maybe you join a new church only to be reminded by the enemy that the last church you attended hurt or disappointed you. If you accept these thoughts as your own you will begin to feel the same way you felt in the past and ultimately engage in the same isolating behavior that characterized that traumatic experience in your past. I see it all the time! Such Christians are haunted.

Usually, they do not attribute offense to anything sinister or demonic and just assume it's the result of natural thoughts and emotions. Nothing could be further from the truth. Offense comes under the category of an "unclean spirit," meaning that this spirit has the unique assignment of defiling the believer and bringing contamination into their spiritual life. Make no mistake, offense contaminates your service, your praise, your relationships, and even your worship.

This is one of the main reasons we become offended: someone (whether knowingly or unknowingly) says or does something that reminds us of a past negative experience. They touch a wounded area in our heart or life. Now, abusive or inappropriate behavior is always unacceptable regardless of past experiences. But the point I'm trying to make is that some behavior can be appropriate and yet entirely upset us. We all have a past. We can't help that. But Satan wants to take what's outside of our control—our past—and use it to mess up what's inside our control—our present.

I believe that God's Word is a "ghostbuster!" He desires to liberate you from the pain of offense so that you can live the abundant life. Offenses will come. But we don't have to be offended.

Vain Imaginations

In order to understand the way offense operates, we must gain a greater insight into imaginations because offenses come from imaginations:

> (For the weapons of our warfare are not carnal, but mighty through God to the pulling down of strong holds;) casting down imaginations, and every high thing that exalts itself against the knowledge of God, and bringing into captivity every thought to the obedience of Christ.
>
> (2 Corinthians 10:4–5)

"Imaginations," as used in this passage, are ways of thinking that are contradictory to God's Word and therefore undermine successful spiritual living. For instance, a person may be hurt deeply by someone close to them and have the thought, *I will never forgive them.* This line of thinking is in direct opposition to God's commandment to forgive.

Why do I refer to them as *vain* imaginations? Because these imaginations are often rooted in pride. When we concentrate on ourselves above God or others, we may be guilty of harboring pride. Much offense comes from our tendency to take everything personally. Do you know that what the devil does to you is not personal? It feels personal but it's not personal. He'll do it to anybody. Can you imagine a burglar walking up to a retiree's house, cracking open the door with a crowbar, grabbing their TV and crystal vase, and a little old lady comes out and says, "Why are you doing this to me? Why me? Why would you break into my house?" And the man says, "Because I'm a criminal, lady! You had the closest house to where I was at and I had to rob somebody!" That's how the devil works.

SATAN'S LIE: YOU'RE AT THE CENTER OF THE DEVIL'S PLAN.
#SPIRITOFOFFENSE

Can you imagine how Jesus felt when Judas Iscariot, someone who had travelled with Him and taught with Him and labored with Him, then went and sold Him just for a bag of coins? Yet Jesus did not take it personally! He knew that it was Satan trying to get in the way of God's plan. We get caught in the crossfire between the devil and God. Remember, the devil is the Accuser of the brethren. *He* is the one who attempts to manipulate your mental space and use your mind for his workshop.

Mind Control

Offenses begin in the mind. And if left intact, they become mental strongholds that perpetuate bondage and defeat. You probably never looked at offenses in this light, but it is absolutely crucial to realize the truth about this extremely serious issue. Offenses begin as thoughts swirling around in our minds. Once we accept the thought as our own, the offense takes root in the heart.

I can remember sitting in a Bible study several years ago, and while the pastor was preaching, I received the thought: *the pastor doesn't like me.* The thought was so persistent and pervasive that I accepted it as a fact. I wondered what I did to the pastor to cause him to dislike me. Every time he glanced at me, I thought, *He sees something in me that he doesn't like....*

Later, I realized that my pastor was not thinking any such thing at all. It was a figment of my imagination. As time went on, I was able to enjoy a healthy and thriving relationship with my pastor because I was willing to say *no* to offense. Do you know that your mind can play tricks on you? Do you know that we can reject people just because we think they're rejecting us? You think somebody doesn't like you. You don't like them, so you assume they don't like you. Guess what? It could all just be in your mind.

WE MUST DISCERN THE DIFFERENCE BETWEEN OUR OWN THOUGHTS AND THE ACCUSATIONS OF THE ENEMY PLANTED IN OUR MIND.

I have experienced this firsthand as a pastor. I cannot tell you the countless times people have accused me of not liking them. They say they can tell by the look on my face. The truth is in most cases I'm not even aware of my facial expressions! I am an expressive person, and sometimes my face is saying what I'm feeling—which has nothing to do with the people in front of me!

Believers get themselves in trouble because they don't recognize that the thought propagating itself in their mind does not come from them. It is your responsibility to interrogate every thought to ensure that it aligns with the Word of God, and if it does not align with the Word of God, you must demolish it! The apostle John told us to try every spirit, to make sure that it was of God. (See 1 John 4:1.) Test the spirits, try them, interrogate them, interview them—*Where did you come from? Who sent you? Why are you in my head? What gave you the authorization to be here? Are you from God? Are you from the devil? Are you from my crazy past? Are you from my trauma? Where did you come from, because I need to know before I accept you as my own!*

If you always ask yourself where the thought is coming from, it will save you from so much pain, so many struggles, and so many difficulties in your life. Before you leave, before you jump ship, before you abort, before you leave that job, before you leave that church, before you leave that relationship, before you do something you'll regret, check yourself. *Is this coming from me?*

One way to tell when a thought is coming from the devil is that when it's seeded by Satan, you cannot justify or explain it. When it's not rational, when you can't quantify or calculate it, when you've put it through a litmus test and it still doesn't come out right, then it's satanic. The devil's a liar. Everything he says is a lie. Everything! Sickness? It's a lie. Bondage? Lie! Poverty? Lie. The Bible says we have to cast down those imaginations. Cast them down. Don't let them sit there too long.

You and I do not have to subject ourselves to negative thought patterns. We can decide to live free and victorious. We can choose to rid ourselves of doubt, suspicion, and fear. Simply put, we can take control of our minds and cast down those vain imaginations. Remember, as a born-again believer, your spirit has jurisdiction over your mind. Just because a thought comes doesn't mean you have to accept it. Many thoughts are sent by the enemy but are masked as our own thoughts, feelings, and emotions. We can defeat them exercising self-control in our minds.

The Battle of the Mind

I have heard it said that the mind is the battlefield of spiritual warfare. Nothing could be more true! Our thoughts affect our heart, and our heart affects our actions, our actions shape our character, and our character determines our destiny. In essence, if we want to change our lives, we must change the way we think. Too many believers are hyper-sensitive and easily offended. Unfortunately, we are encouraged in the Western world to believe that our feelings and our emotions are of the ultimate importance. But the truth is that the Bible gives a very different hierarchy. The most important thing to a Christian is God's Word—aka, the truth. Once we reconcile in our heart and mind that God's truth is the final authority for our lives, we can begin to see victory.

You must understand that strongholds are inhabited by demonic forces. Satan lives within the framework of negative thought patterns. Many Christians have housed the devil in a high-rise apartment in their minds. He is not even paying any rent!

Recently, I was driving past what was once a very large building and realized that the building had been torn down. The demolition crew came and destroyed this building during the night. One moment it was there, the next moment it was gone. This is the word picture of when the Bible tells us to cast down imaginations. Instead of "casting down," imagine a demolition crew wrecking the building of your vain imaginations. The Bible tells us to demolish every mental stronghold and to destroy every imagination that seeks to exalt itself above the knowledge of God. How do we accomplish this feat? Simply put, the Word of God is our wrecking ball. Through God's Word, we break ungodly thought patterns rooted in offense.

SATAN'S LIE:
IT'S OK TO DAILY RELIVE YOUR
PAIN, HURT, AND DISAPPOINTMENT.
#SPIRITOFOFFENSE

For years I suffered from the debilitating effects of offense in my heart. Anytime I talked about the situation that had caused the offense, I noticed that the pain would emerge and feel just as real as it was the day it transpired. One day the Lord spoke to me and asked, "Why do you continue to rehearse painful experiences?" Honestly, until then, I never really thought about what I was doing. In fact, I would even spiritualize this negative practice. I would think, *I'm just talking about my experiences.* But the truth was that I was erecting an ungodly structure in my mind.

God was telling me that it was time to tear down the old house of hurt, pain, trauma, negative experiences, and bitterness so that He could build a new house. A house of peace, joy, grace, love, and favor. It was time to change addresses. It was time to move from 666 Barely Get Along Street to 777 Victory Lane. We accomplish this is by meditating in the Word of God. By *meditate*, I do not mean going to a Buddhist temple or taking up tai chi or yoga. Biblical meditation involves thinking about, speaking, or muttering God's Word to yourself over and over again. We have to renew our minds with the Word of God. As Paul said,

I beseech you therefore, brethren, by the mercies of God, that you present your bodies a living sacrifice, holy, acceptable to God, which is your reasonable service. And be not conformed to this world: but be you transformed by the renewing of your mind, that you may prove what is that good, and acceptable, and perfect, will of God.

(Romans 12:1–2)

The more we meditate on the Word of God, the more power and momentum we give to the spiritual battering ram that has the power to demolish mental strongholds.

Hallelujah!

The Prison of Offense

The enemy always uses an occurrence, situation, or hurt to draw us into his evil plot. The victim often does not even recognize that they have been drawn into a trap until it is too late. For example, I can remember a particular situation in which a person in my church was under the impression that I was speaking about them in my sermons. You would be surprised by how often this happens! As a result, they began to distance themselves from me and from other people in the church. They thought, *The pastor is talking about me from the pulpit—how could he do such a thing?* They began to make judgments and assessments based upon their perception of what was really happening. Eventually, they left the church.

How could something so seemingly trivial cause someone to make such a serious decision? It is not about what happened, but the way it was perceived. *Offense* can be defined as an annoyance or resentment brought about by a perceived insult to or disregard for oneself or one's standards or principles. The person was vexed and annoyed by what they perceived to be a personal attack against their character. Ironically, I was not even speaking about them. Later, the person came back and expressed their grievance, and the situation was rectified. But at what cost?

Years ago I watched a movie, which became a favorite of mine, called *The Hurricane* and starring Denzel Washington. Based on a true story, the movie depicts a boxer nicknamed "The Hurricane" who was falsely accused of murder and imprisoned for many years. While in prison, the boxer found enlightenment and began to write compelling books from his cell. A young man from Canada read his books and decided to go on a campaign to exonerate the falsely accused boxer. In one very emotional scene, the young man is frustrated that their appeal was unsuccessful and the boxer is still in prison, and says to Denzel Washington's character, "We are going to bust you out of here!" Denzel Washington peacefully responds, "Hate put me in prison, but *love* is going to bust me out!"

OFFENSE IS NOT JUST A NEGATIVE EMOTION; IT IS AN EVIL SPIRIT WHOSE ASSIGNMENT IS TO KEEP YOU BOUND.

This scene reminds me of so many people in the church today. Offense is more than a mere emotional reaction to hurt, it is a spirit that produces bondage. Countless believers have been sentenced to a prison of offense and bitterness as a result of accepting the false accusations, lies, and deceptions of the enemy.

How many people have never rectified the pain and hurt they are feeling, but rather go on in a resentful state? How many are adding a bar to their prison every day by dwelling on a problem that was really just a misunderstanding? How many wonderful servants of God are sitting in prisons that the church helped to make—or at least didn't warn against?

Beloved, this is not the will of God. We must be vigilant to not give the enemy any place in our lives. We must guard our hearts against taking offense, and we must seek reconciliation with each other when offense has been taken. Offense may have imprisoned you, but the love and power of God is going to bust you out in the name of Jesus!

Breaking the Spirit of Offense

How do we break the spirit of offense? We will flesh this out more fully in future chapters, but here are three important steps.

Forgive

Forgiveness breaks the power of offense. The gospel of Luke tells us in chapter 17: *"If your brother trespass against you, rebuke him; and if he repent, forgive him"* (verse 3). The Scripture further tells us that we should forgive without keeping a record of how many times we have forgiven!

Jesus told Peter to forgive *"seventy times seven"* (Matthew 18:22). This doesn't mean that you go to 490 times, then quit! No, it symbolically means you forgive into infinity.

The problem in the church is that we don't really forgive. We keep people in limbo. It's not the same as forgiving. Essentially, we're saying, "I'm going to give you a conditional contract. I am going to be nice toward you, but if you act up again, I'm going to shut you out." Now God, in all His mercy and grace, doesn't levy the same stipulation toward us. Sometimes you ask God to forgive you for the same thing a hundred times and yet He never rejects you when you come to Him again. He is so compassionate and loving. He has the ability to forget stuff. Now you don't have the same omniscience as God to *forget* things, but you can let stuff go.

SATAN'S LIE:
IF YOU CAN'T FORGET IT,
YOU CAN'T FORGIVE IT EITHER.
#SPIRITOFOFFENSE

That's what it means; the word *forgive* means "to release." You need to let it go. Stop holding on to stuff that happened to you twenty years ago. That's gone. Your yesterday has nothing to do with your today! If that wasn't the case, all of us would be disqualified; but because we serve a God that is unconditional in His grace, He does not limit us to what we did yesterday. He says, with each morning sun, "I am going to give you a brand new day with a brand new mercy and a brand new opportunity to serve Me today."

Many women have been messed up because of what has happened to them in the past. I am here to tell you that according to God's Word, your past does not define you. I don't care what happened to you or who was involved or what the motives were, you are the daughter of the King and there is nothing that the devil can do to disqualify you from who God says you are: treasured royalty.

The Bible says in Ephesians 4:32: *"And be you kind one to another, tender-hearted, forgiving one another, even as God for Christ's sake has forgiven you.*" Notice that God's forgiveness toward you wasn't based on your behavior. It was based on Christ. And your forgiveness of others is not based on their behavior. It's based on Christ. When you tell someone you forgive them, you're saying, "I'm forgiving you not because you deserve to be forgiven but because God commands me to forgive and I'm not going to be messed up with your stuff while I'm here."

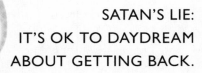

SATAN'S LIE:
IT'S OK TO DAYDREAM
ABOUT GETTING BACK.
#SPIRITOFOFFENSE

Repent

Repentance also breaks through the power of offense. It is the Greek word *metanoia*, and it means "to change your mind; think differently; to turn." You have to turn from yesterday and turn to the Word of God. First off, we've got to repent for harboring offense. We have to say:

"Lord, forgive me for holding on to vain imaginations to begin with."

"God, I ask You to cleanse me of this."

"Lord, I have harbored things in my heart that are not right. They don't glorify You. They don't honor You."

"Lord, I've made an idol out of my hurt."

What? An *idol*? Yes! We can make an idol out of our hurt. An idol is anything that we put in place of God. When we let our hurts dictate our actions, thoughts, and feelings, instead of letting God's Word dictate our lives, then our hurt is our idol! And the Scripture tells us, *"Have no other gods before Me"* (Exodus 20:3). He says repent. Repent and be cleansed. The Scripture is so powerful. We can pray with King David, *"Wash me thoroughly from my iniquity, and cleanse me from my sin.… Make me to hear joy and gladness; that the bones which You have broken may rejoice"* (Psalm 51:2, 8).

When you hold on to grudges and offenses in your heart, you give the one who offended you control over you. In biblical days, when someone committed certain crimes—heinous crimes—they would attach a corpse to the person and the person would have to travel around with this corpse for days. As the corpse decomposed, the decomposition became poisonous to the living person's body. Ultimately, the one carrying the dead man died himself. That's how offense is. It's like having a dead man attached to you. It doesn't kill you instantly, but it does kill you slowly. It's a slow assassination. That's why you've got to forgive. You've got to repent.

We have to be vigilant and intentional in silencing the voice of the enemy that is reminding you of what happened yesterday. Stop letting the devil remind you of your failures and your faults! You have to put yourself in the space of just thanking God. Say, "God, though I messed up yesterday, I thank You, Lord, that Your grace is sufficient for today and, God, I receive Your power—to step into my destiny."

Avoid

"Now I beseech you, brethren, mark them which cause divisions and offenses contrary to the doctrine which you have learned; and avoid them" (Romans 16:17). Paul the apostle admonished the church in Rome to mark those which cause offenses among the church and to avoid them. The word *mark* conveys an interesting idea. Paul was telling the church to watch out for people who spread offense. Why? Because offense is like a spiritual disease that can infect people on contact.

I want you to imagine that you are walking down a dark alley, and you can't see the ground beneath you. You are on your way to your destination, and all of a sudden you trip over something, but you can't see what it is. You fall to the ground in pain, trying to figure out what it was that caused you to trip. This is the way offense operates; it causes the believers who subject themselves to it to stumble. The problem is that most believers don't know what they are stumbling over. Can you imagine living your Christian life always being frustrated and never reaching your fullest potential? Always walking in the dark, tripping over obstacles? Always feeling like something is missing from your life, and never being able to identify what that "something" really is?

The enemy of our soul does not want us to flourish and prosper in the things of God, so he often manipulates us into looking at the circumstances of our lives and becoming offended at the things we go through.

Unfortunately, the church has become a breeding ground for offense. It doesn't matter how big or how small the offense is, if you allow offenses to persist they will cause you to fall. Thank God we have a promise from the Word of God: *"Now to Him that is able to keep you from falling, and to present you faultless before the presence of His glory with exceeding joy"* (Jude 24).

Many people have been spiritually abused in the church, and I will deal with that in more detail a little later. But leaders must also guard their heart against offense. One of the most toxic things in the body of Christ is an offended leader. This is why it is important for leaders to maintain a proper perspective as it relates to the sheep God has given them leadership over. The moment you become retaliatory in your dealings with people under your leadership, that's the moment you run the risk of destroying their morale and discouraging their faith walk.

Your kingdom assignment is for you to move forward and upward. Anything that causes you to be stagnant or to stumble is not from God. I repeat, it is not from God!

For Discussion

1. Why is offense inevitable?

2. Why is the *mind* the battlefield of spiritual warfare, and not the heart, the church, the street, the workplace, or the home? Have you experienced spiritual warfare in your thoughts?

3. What are the three important steps to breaking the power of offense?

Testimony

After enduring a very nasty divorce, I was so bitter. The doctors diagnosed me with rheumatoid arthritis. For years I suffered in pain and agony and eventually realized that I would probably have to live in pain for the rest of my life. One night I came to a service where Dr. Kynan was teaching. He told us to release the pain of our past. I asked the

Lord to help me to forgive my ex-husband, and as I prayed the prayer of release that night, something lifted off of me. I literally felt lighter! I knew that something had changed in my body. The next day, I went to the doctor and they could not find any rheumatoid inflammation. The pain went away, and I experienced the healing power of God. I stopped allowing the Accuser to sow bitterness and anger into my heart, and finally said *no* to offense. Praise God!

—*Anonymous*

Prayer

Father, in the name of Jesus, I thank You for who You are and all that You have done in my life. Father, I recognize that offense is a spirit that does not come from You. I take authority over the spirit of offense and command it to leave every area of my life. I refuse to operate in a spirit of offense. I freely forgive all of those who have offended, hurt, or wounded me. I break the power of offense off of my life and the lives of my loved ones. I recognize that my kingdom assignment is more important than offense. I cast down every vain imagination and demolish every mental stronghold. Every negative thought must leave me now. Father, teach me to honor You in my thought life and with my words. I will live free from all bondage in my life. In the name of Jesus!

Amen.

6
DON'T TAKE THE BAIT

Now I beseech you, brethren, mark them which cause divisions and offenses contrary to the doctrine which you have learned; and avoid them. (Romans 16:17)

When I was a kid, we lived in a house with a huge basement. And at some point, my father discovered that the basement was infested with rats. Though there weren't many, they were *big*. What do you do when you find out you have a rat? You buy a rattrap, of course! My father purchased a state-of-the-art trap supposedly guaranteed to work in all conditions. It really just looked like a little tent with a floor made of glue. The idea was to spread a cheesy mixture at the entrance to the tent to attract the rat. When the rat walks in to eat the cheese, it gets stuck and eventually—hopefully—suffocates.

Well, one afternoon I heard a scurrying sound in the basement, and I figured we had caught our first rat. Excited, I ran to the trap and lifted the top. A huge rat, not yet stuck, lunged straight up and took a huge bite out of my finger. I dropped that trap just as fast as I could and ran away screaming. That was one of the most painful and frightening experiences of my life!

To say I hate rats and rattraps now would be an understatement. But the years between me and the experience have given me another insight, too. If this was terrifying for me, I can only imagine what the rat was feeling. Can you imagine the fear and anxiety of knowing that you were stuck forever just because you ate some cheese? Was it really worth it? If he had ever got out, I can guarantee you that the rat would never have taken the same bait twice.

Many Christians, like that rat in the basement, have taken the bait of offense and found themselves trapped in a suffocating hold of hurt, pain, and disappointment. They scurry around grasping for air as the apparatus of Satan closes in on their soul. I have counseled countless people who have found themselves stuck in their spiritual lives because they took the bait.

I have been trapped before and know what is like to be bound. How did I escape? I will answer that question in just a moment, but I first want to explore the bait of offense a little further.

The Carnal Appetite

Why did the rat go after the cheese? Why was he so drawn to its taste? The reason is the same as why human beings are prone to being offended: both have developed a carnal appetite for it. The Bible says, *"For they that are after the flesh do mind the things of the flesh; but they that are after the Spirit the things of the Spirit"* (Romans 8:5). The desiring of things *"after the flesh"* is crucial to understanding why offense contains such an allure for believers.

The term *"after the flesh"* denotes motion or direction. In other words, those who pursue carnal thoughts, desires, and appetites will set their mind on such things. An appetite is a natural desire to satisfy a bodily need, especially for food. The more of a thing we eat, the more we desire to eat it! It's like a kid who wants nothing but mac'n'cheese because he eats nothing but mac'n'cheese. The same is true of offense: the more we engage in it, the more we will be allured by it.

Have you ever had someone come up to you and ask, "Did you hear what John Doe said about you?" I'll bet my bottom dollar that you were instantly interested! But it is your carnal nature that is drawn to the knowledge apart from God. Just as the Tree of Knowledge of Good and Evil seduced Eve, so many are seduced by knowledge that we are not supposed to have. There is a part of us that is easily swayed by the notion of being offended.

There was a recent study that suggested that Americans were the most stressed population on the planet. Why? I wonder if it's because we actually *enjoy* being stressed. Many people have an appetite for anger, road rage, frustration, and displeasure. In fact, if they are not a little irritated about one thing or another, they believe something is wrong.

So what is the solution? We must change our appetite! How do we change our appetite? We change our appetite by changing what we eat. Instead of entertaining the voices of fear, hurt, and anger, we must embrace a healthy diet of God's Word. The Bible says, *"Finally, brethren, whatsoever things are true, whatsoever things are honest, whatsoever things are just, whatsoever things are pure, whatsoever things are lovely, whatsoever things are of good report; if there be any virtue, and if there be any praise, think on these things"* (Philippians 4:8).

The Expense of Offense

In the Bible, we read a very interesting story about two brothers named Esau and Jacob. They were technically twins, but because Esau cane out of the womb first, he was considered the eldest brother. In the culture of the time, the eldest son was entitled to the birthright—the privilege one has from birth including the promised inheritance of land, material possessions, and spiritual blessings. The birthright was a very serious thing! You would think that Esau would make sure his birthright was kept safe. But listen to what happened:

> *And the boys grew: and Esau was a cunning hunter, a man of the field; and Jacob was a plain man, dwelling in tents.... And Jacob sod pottage* [made stew]: *and Esau came from the field, and he was faint: and Esau said to Jacob, Feed me, I pray you, with that same red pottage; for I am faint: therefore was his name called Edom. And Jacob said, Sell me this day your birthright. And Esau said, Behold, I am at the point to die: and what profit shall this birthright do to me? And Jacob said, Swear to me this day; and he sware to him: and he sold his birthright to Jacob. Then Jacob gave Esau bread and pottage of lentils; and he did eat and drink, and rose up, and went his way: thus Esau despised his birthright.* (Genesis 25:27, 29–34)

The Bible says that Jacob offered Esau stew in exchange for his birthright. Clearly these were not things of equal value, yet in Esau's hunger and desperation he offered up something of great worth in exchange for a piece of meat. This is a perfect illustration of how the enemy of our souls deceives us out of our spiritual blessings by convincing us that our right to be offended is more important that the "birthright" that God has made available to every one of His children. We exchange the short-term gratification of feeling offended for the long-term reward of inheriting the kingdom of heaven.

It is often said that we should never make a serious decision on an empty stomach and instead make sure that we have a balanced meal. The same is true of spiritual things. We must make sure that we are not spiritually empty before acting on a decision that will cost us our birthright. Too many believers are selling their spiritual birthrights for one morsel of offense. It is never worth the cost. Jacob could not take it by force, but he could supplant it through deception. ("Jacob" means *supplanted*.) The enemy of our souls is likewise constantly trying to supplant the promises of God in your life.

Recently, I heard a story of a man who received a watch from his uncle. It was an old, beat-up Rolex that his uncle bought in 1965. The watch didn't look like much; it had scratches and other dents all over its face. This man figured he would send it back to the manufacturer to repair it and then sell it. He sent the watch to New York City to be serviced. While the watch was en route, he visited a jeweler and told them about his recent acquisition. Out of curiosity he asked for an appraisal. His eyes bulged when he discovered that his uncle's beat-up Rolex was now valued at $75,000. His uncle had initially bought the watch for nearly $300 and its value was now 250 times that. He immediately contacted the manufacturer and told them not to repair it—because opening the case would depreciate the value of the watch.

This guy hadn't realized the value of what he possessed, and so he was willing to send it away in the hopes of making some quick cash. The Bible says that the thief comes to steal, kill, and destroy. (See John 10:10.) It is important to realize the devil is *always* in the business of stealing from us. How does he steal? He steals from believers by convincing us to give up something of great value in exchange for something of little to no value. Your peace of mind is more valuable than an expensive Rolex watch! But if you don't realize its value, you may let it go for the sake of the short-term gratification of being angry or offended. I am here to tell you that the devil intends to steal your joy and your peace and you must make up your mind to give him no place!

The question you must ask yourself is this: What will it cost me? How expensive is this offense? How damaging will this conversation be to my spiritual life? Greater things await for all who return love for hurt and patience for malevolence.

SATAN'S LIE:
IF YOU'RE A CHRISTIAN,
IT'S YOUR JOB TO BE OFFENSIVE.
#DONTTAKETHEBAIT

Offended Versus Offensive

Now I want us to quickly explore the distinction between being *offended* and being *offensive*. The Bible tells us in the book of Hebrews that Esau was a fornicator and that he sold his birthright for one morsel of meat. (See Hebrews 12:16–17.) It also says that he found no place of repentance though he sought it desperately with tears. In other words, Esau succumbed to the lustful desires of his flesh. When the Bible talks about lust it is not always talking about sexual lust, but is sometimes referring to a lust for power, for control, even for food or drink! Esau was so hungry that he couldn't see the situation clearly, succumbed to his desire, and lived to regret it. Bitterness spoke into his heart, and he determined to kill his brother. (See Genesis 27:41.)

This is how many believers graduate from being offended to being offensive. Beloved, we must not allow ourselves to be oversensitive and do the devil's work for him. We must learn from Esau to be careful not to allow our offense to cause us to become offensive. Once you internalize the offense, rest assured that eventually it will be externalized. Offense is like an attacking military campaign.

There are many people in the body of Christ who have succumbed to an offensive spirit, and as a result they go around attacking everyone in their path. They attack pastors, they attack churches, and they attack other believers. Most of them don't even realize that they are the perpetrators of this heinous behavior. Furthermore, they don't recognize that it is the Accuser of the brethren behind it all.

SOMETIMES THE MOST OFFENDED PEOPLE ARE THE MOST OFFENSIVE PEOPLE.

It is good to have a healthy level of self-examination in one's life to avoid this. Once I counseled a man who was struggling in his relationships with other people in the church. He wondered why people were always mistreating him. One day, I stopped to watch his interactions some of the other parishioners. He was being very rude and brash. I then realized that his problem was not being *offended* (per se), but the fact that he was very *offensive* in his words and actions. I believe that more people fall under this category of behavior than we realize. This is why the Word of God and an intimate relationship with the Holy Spirit are critical when it comes to gaining lasting victory over offense. Don't dish out what you are incapable of receiving. Do unto others as you would have them to do unto you.

Can I be completely honest here with the ministers and leaders? *Please* make sure that you are not ministering out of offense. There are too many leaders who are operating out of a wounded soul. Allow the Lord to bring healing to those areas so that your ministry will not be contaminated by dysfunction. Do not become a King Saul to someone else!

Beware of Offense Brokers

Let me flashback to high school economics class and the principle of supply and demand to explain my next point: the greater the demand, the greater the supply will be to meet the demand. The same is true of offense. Because the church has had an appetite for offense, there has been no shortage of offended people. In fact, there are people in the church whom I refer to as offense brokers.

A broker is someone who buys and sells goods or assets for others, or someone who arranges or negotiates something. Offense brokers are those in the church who are readily available to assist you in your offense transaction.

For instance, if the pastor or leadership say something hurtful or offensive, the offense brokers will be at your beck and call to assist you in your wounding. "The pastor should not have said that to you...." "The leadership seems to be doing that to everybody...." "I can't believe that actually happened!" On the outside they may seem to be helpful and harmless, but in reality they are extremely hazardous. It is very dangerous to your spiritual health to be surrounded by people who help you to become more and more offended.

I was speaking to a fellow church member one day who began to tell me what someone else had said about me. They were very articulate in their narration, leaving no stone left unturned. The more they divulged, the more hurt and angry I became. I didn't realize that I should have stopped them before they even started. At the time I didn't realize that this person was far from a friend. I never thought to ask them what *they* said to the other person about *me* when I wasn't in the room.

IF THEY WILL TALK WITH YOU ABOUT SOMEONE ELSE, THEY WILL TALK WITH SOMEONE ELSE ABOUT YOU!

This person was an offense broker. Their assignment was to get me to operate in the flesh rather than to walk in the Spirit. They were not a friend, because a friend does not dwell in or report false words. A true friend will defend you in your absence and encourage you in your presence. A true friend is a broker of hope and healing, rather than a broker of hurt and heartache. Yet too often, our friends are more willing to talk about the most recent scandal or gossip rather than speak into our lives the purpose of God.

The Abomination of Discord

One of the most memorable passages of Scripture I have ever read is found in the book of Proverbs (also referred to as the Book of Wisdom). As a side note, I think everyone should read at least one chapter from Proverbs every day for an increased level of success in life and relationships. Listen to this wisdom:

These six things does the LORD hate: yea, seven are an abomination to Him: a proud look, a lying tongue, and hands that shed innocent blood, a heart that devises wicked imaginations, feet that be swift in running to mischief, a false witness that speaks lies, and he that sows discord among brethren. (Proverbs 6:16–19)

"Six things that God hates, and the seventh is an abomination." This is very strong language! An *abomination* is defined as something that causes disgust or deep hatred. You would think that an abomination would be something like adultery, bestiality, or some other sexually perverse act. (Those things are listed as abominations in other passages but not here.) No! Here, the abomination is *"he that sows discord among brethren!"* You mean to tell me that discord among brethren is an abomination in the sight of God? Absolutely! God hates strife and division, and He does not wink at those who participate in such behavior.

WHERE THERE IS DISCORD, THERE IS STRIFE AND EVERY EVIL WORK OF THE ENEMY!

Why is God so serious about discord? Because everything about His kingdom is based upon unity and harmony. You will never find the Trinity having a disagreement. You will never see angels arguing with each other. (Actually, an angel tried that once and it didn't go over too well!) Everything in creation works in harmony, and when there is dissonance, it causes natural disasters. The Bible says, *"For where envying and strife is, there is confusion and every evil work"* (James 3:16). Strife, confusion, and discord are the atmosphere of evil. This atmosphere invites Satan and his demons to operate. God knows that His presence cannot thrive in this type of environment, and this is why He despises discord so much.

The Hebrew root word for *discord* also implies *judge* or *vindicator*. God knows that He is the only One who fulfills that role successfully and He hates it when we try to step into His position. When we engage in strife and discord we are acting like Lucifer. He attempted to ascend to a position that did not belong to him. Let us not follow his example! Instead, we should endeavor to keep the unity of the Spirit in the bond of peace. (See Ephesians 4:3.)

Noticing the Seeds of Discord

Notice that the Bible doesn't say discord is *created*, the Bible says it is *"sown."* Discord begins as a seed and that seed produces a harvest. How do we sow discord among brethren? Through the words that we speak. I have found in my experience as a Christian that most grievances and offenses are initiated and exacerbated by words.

One time many years ago, a young woman in our church felt slighted by my wife because my wife was quite introverted at the time and did not talk much. In a vindictive spirit, this woman made some strong accusations against me. Through these false accusations, she managed to pit us against the leadership of the church and intended to cause confusion between me and my wife. In a situation like that, one might feel justified in attacking such a person and counter-slandering them or maybe even exposing them publically them as a liar. But instead, we stayed quiet and maintained our peace. Later we requested mediation with one of the associated pastors and the accuser. After all was settled and her statements were exposed as false, we embraced her and showed Christ's love.

It was not easy. In fact, it was one of the hardest things we had ever done. Soon after, the Lord used my wife to minister healing and restoration to the same young woman who had once tried to defame us. The devil failed! Though God intervened supernaturally, it was the plan of the enemy to divide and conquer. This is how discord works. A seed was sown in the form of an accusation and this seed was harvested as strife and confusion. Thankfully God canceled the harvest!

I pray that the Lord would cancel the plans of the enemy in your life as well. I speak crop failure to every seed of strife, confusion, and discord in your life in the name of Jesus!

Differentiating Discord from Disagreement

Contrary to popular opinion, nothing we say is harmless. Every word we speak (even idle words) has an exponential effect on the people and situations around us. As believers, we do not have the right to express ourselves however we want. I don't mean that we cannot disagree! Nowhere in the Bible does God condone brainwashing. We have the right to disagree, but we do not have the right to sow discord. In our church, we encourage people to think for themselves and to dialogue about differences of opinions, but they must do so in a way that honors God and their fellow brothers and sisters. Seeds of discord are more than simple statements of disagreement. They are negative statements about leadership or other church members that are not redemptive or honoring.

For example, when new people come to our church who are not first-time churchgoers, I like to ask them what their past experiences with church were like. If they say, "My last pastor was horrible. He didn't follow the Holy Spirit, and he didn't do what the Bible said," I immediately know that there is a seed within that could potentially cause problems because that statement does not sound full of grace and peace!

SATAN'S LIE: IF YOU DON'T 100% AGREE, YOU SHOULD LEAVE.

#DONTTAKETHEBAIT

Now I understand that there are many situations where people need to leave and there may be much hurt in the process, but those who are sincerely seeking to please God must be careful to speak in a manner that is redemptive and honoring. If anybody needs help overcoming pain or abuse, they should always be encouraged to seek godly counsel.

It can be very difficult to resist, especially when you are experiencing hurt or pain, but I have learned that on the other side of pain is promotion: *"If the spirit of the ruler rise up against you, leave not your place; for yielding pacifies great offenses"* (Ecclesiastes 10:4). What if I told you that with every test you underwent was a testimony? I know it sounds very cliché—but it is absolutely true.

The Vagabond Spirit

A dear pastor friend of mine called me and told me about a situation in his church. He was planting a new church in a new city and was very excited. But one Sunday, after a powerful service, a man came up to him, fixed him with an intense glare, and informed him that there are no such things as pastors in the Bible. My friend shook his head in amazement.

He didn't know what to say, so he called me and asked me about it. I told him that the man in question was likely trouble.

Later, it was discovered that this same man began to hold meetings with other people in the church and accuse the pastor of spiritual incompetence. He told others that the pastor doesn't preach the Bible the way he should. Ultimately, this gentleman left the church and took some people with him. This is a very tragic story; yet it happens far too often.

People like the man in this story are what I call spiritual vagabonds. As a result of hurt, rejection, and pain at a particular point in their spiritual development, spiritual vagabonds have embraced a negative, cynical, and often adversarial attitude toward the church. Like a natural vagabond who wanders from place to place without a home or job, spiritual vagabonds wander from church to church never settling in or establishing their roots in the house of God. They quite often have a persona of hyper-spirituality, but deep within they are hyper-sensitive and prone to offense. At the first sign of disagreement from the pastor or the members, they leave. If the pastor corrects them, they leave. If they see something that doesn't fit into their preconceived notion of what the church should be, they leave!

SPIRITUAL VAGABONDS ARE NOT BORN; THEY ARE MADE THAT WAY AS A RESULT OF HURT.

Unfortunately, these individuals never receive healing and wholeness, because they refuse to submit to or to become a part of community long enough to get the breakthrough.

In most cases, these people have been to several churches and each time it turned out like the last. Either the pastor said something offensive, or they "discerned" that something was out of order in the church. As a pastor once said, "There is no such thing as a perfect church, and if you find one, it won't be perfect after you join!" However, spiritual vagabonds go about sowing discord from church to church, obsessing over the imperfections they find, instead of pursuing peace and spiritual growth. On the other hand, when church members eagerly pursue understanding, there will be unity and the realization that we are all one unit working toward the same result: the advancement of the kingdom of God. Discord and division will never thrive in an atmosphere of unity and spiritual maturity.

Offense Gets Us Nowhere

Back in the Bible days, and even sometimes today, they had what is called a "fowler." A fowler was a person who hunted birds. He would put a trap on the ground, put food inside it, and rig it with a little mechanism so that when the bird came near the bait, the bird would trigger a trap stick and be trapped. He was bound. He was locked up. He was confined and eventually he died.

The word *offense* comes from the Greek word *scandalon*, which can also mean *bait trap*. Offense is the bait of Satan. It is the trap stick of the enemy that causes you and me to stumble prematurely. It can cause as person to be bound up so they cannot fulfill their calling and purpose. This is why the spirit of offense has been running rampant in the church. The enemy knows that if he can trap people in its clutches, he can render them ineffective in their assignment.

If we recognized that offense was the bait of Satan, we would be careful not to be so easily offended. Are you listening to what I am saying? We are living in a time in history where we need to exercise more vigilance than ever before, because the Accuser of the brethren is lurking in the dark places waiting to take advantage of our hurt, pain, and disappointment. Now I'm not trying to glorify him, but he is busy; he is working; he is exploiting every crack and crevice of your life. He wants you to succumb to your carnal appetites, become offensive, sow discord, and turn into a spiritual vagabond. Beloved, offense gets us nowhere. Let's stop.

For Discussion

1. Have you personally experienced offense turning into offensiveness? Describe. What's the solution?

2. What does discord look like in the church? What seeds does it usually grow from?

3. Is every church member who moves around a "vagabond"? Why or why not? What are some symptoms of being a spiritual vagabond?

Practicum

1. What difficult things in your past might be holding you back? Begin the process of breaking free by verbalizing your hurt to God, then declaring that you are a *"new creation"* in Christ, according to 2 Corinthians 5:17. How can you live out the rest of this powerful passage?

> *Therefore, if anyone is in Christ, he is a new creation. The old has passed away; behold, the new has come. All this is from God, who through Christ reconciled us to himself and gave us the ministry of reconciliation; that is, in Christ God was reconciling the world to himself, not counting their trespasses against them, and entrusting to us the message of reconciliation. Therefore, we are ambassadors for Christ, God making his appeal through us. We implore you on behalf of Christ, be reconciled to God.*
>
> (2 Corinthians 5:17–20 ESV)

2. Identify areas of offense in your life and walk through the three steps: a) Who am I supposed to forgive? b) What am I supposed to repent of? c) How can I avoid this in the future?

3. Not taking Satan's bait involves us examining our true motives at all times because if we don't, we risk walking straight into his trap. Decide today to always look inward and discern why you are doing and saying something. Ask yourself whether it feeds and satisfies your spiritual appetite or your carnal appetite. Make the commitment to not be the person who sows discord, but the person who sows peace as a child of God is supposed to. (See Matthew 5:9.) Write out the definitions of discord and peace, and make a list of ways you will plant the latter, and not the former, going forward.

Testimony

My pastor recently taught us how to recognize the origins of and overcome the spirit of anger. Before that message, I never thought I was struggling with anger, and I definitely didn't know it was a battle that I had been losing for years. I used to think an angry person always lashed out, was just rude and obnoxious, and had an attitude problem. I didn't see myself like that at all. I was quiet, standoffish, and slow to speak. There were many times when my mood would switch from happy to sad or annoyed very quickly, but I told myself it was because I wasn't where I wanted or thought I should be in life—mentally, financially, spiritually, and emotionally.

I knew I was discontent, dissatisfied, and emotionally unstable, but the message the pastor taught us made me realize that I was actually very *angry*, with myself. He explained that anger is rooted in unmet needs, unfulfilled emotions, self-centeredness, pride, lack of self-control, and toxic emotions, and that anger agitates the soul. That certainly hit home for me, because as I thought about all that I had been through and caused, and the opportunities I missed or turned my back on, I couldn't help but admit that I was dealing with all of those symptoms, and my soul was most definitely disturbed.

And at the root of all of that was offense.

I was offended that other people had more than me or were more spiritually mature than me, even though I was getting the same information from the Bible and in church that they were. And I was offended at myself for not being more outgoing and ambitious. And I was offended that I was offended! That's crazy, isn't it? However, making a practice of looking inwardly, as God's Word tells us to do, and of examining myself and my own motives and intentions, has caused me to experience peace and freedom that I never felt when I refused to look at me. It is an ongoing, daily practice, and I will never go back to living my life trapped inside the cage of offense. —*Anonymous*

Prayer

Father, in the name of Jesus, according to Your Word, I declare that I am vigilant and sober against the devil who walks about as a roaring lion, seeking whom he may devour. I stand on the promise of Your Word, which says that no weapon formed against me will be able to prosper. I refuse to participate in any form of slander and gossip. I refuse to open my heart to the Accuser of the brethren. Instead, I choose to be accountable to the Word of God. From this day forward, I will walk in the nature of Christ. I will operate in the spirit of forgiveness.

Amen.

7

A MORE EXCELLENT WAY

Moreover if your brother shall trespass against you, go and tell him his fault between you and him alone: if he shall hear you, you have gained your brother. But if he will not hear you, then take with you one or two more, that in the mouth of two or three witnesses every word may be established. (Matthew 18:15–16)

There is a more excellent way to respond to sin than to be offended! Even when you are the victim of slander or gossip, you have a different option than simply withdrawing in offense and bitterness. The Bible says that when your brother trespasses against you, rebuke him, and if he repents, forgive him. What it doesn't say is if your brother trespasses against you, go and tell your other brother what they did to you. That is *not* sanctioned in Scripture and only perpetuates the sin!

First Things First

If I told the average Christian that they were in rebellion against God, I would probably be met with a very adversarial response. Something like, "How dare you claim that I am in rebellion?" But it's true! Most Christians rebel against the Word of God in their *relationships*. Jesus was very clear in His instruction to the church. He said that if our brother or sister trespass against us, we are to go to that person. Do you know that many people violate the Word of God in this area? How many, instead of going to the one who offended them, go to a third party first?

There is a protocol that we must follow when it comes to dealing with offenses. The first thing that God tells us to do is to go directly to the one who offended us. Why? Because by doing so, we give the person who has offended us the opportunity to address the offense head-on. I have found that in most cases when we take this first step, we find that the offense was never really an offense at all. It was simply the result of a misunderstanding or miscommunication.

Some time ago, during a busy season, I asked my wife to help me with a particular project, but I quickly became dissatisfied with the level of help I was receiving from her. I became angry and frustrated. I felt that I was being neglected. I was offended. One day, in my frustration, I began to complain to my wife and ask her why she didn't help me on this particular project. She then began to explain to me that she was overwhelmed; the daily routine of school, work, children, and all the other ministry responsibilities were very difficult to balance. It wasn't a matter of not wanting to help me, it was a matter of trying to balance all of her other responsibilities.

EVERY TIME WE BRING OUR GRIEVANCE TO THE PERSON WHO OFFENDED US PRIVATELY, WE GIVE GOD THE OPPORTUNITY TO BRING HEALING AND WHOLENESS.

I realized that it was not a matter of offense, it was a matter of miscommunication. I was not taking into consideration all the things on her plate. Instead, I was selfishly focusing on what I needed in the moment. In her efforts to be supportive, she didn't want to complain about her responsibilities even though she was overwhelmed. I could have loved my wife much better by talking with her at the start instead of becoming angry and offended.

If someone offends you, go to them and tell them about it. Express what you are feeling or have felt. Don't hold it in your heart and sit around mad, hurt, and rejected. By the grace of God, you all can sit down and break bread and fellowship and get beyond the situation to something else! If you're offended with your spouse, tell him or her. Your going to bed mad not wanting to talk, giving each other the silent treatment—it's all nonsense, childishness, and immaturity.

The Scripture says that if your brother trespass against you, you must go to that brother! But we tend to do the opposite. We violate Scripture, we go our own way, and then we wonder why circumstances and situations are compromised or out of order. We need to understand that we cannot violate God's order. There's a reason why God told you to go to the person when you're offended with them: it's because God is always interested in restoration.

When God has a problem with you, He goes to you. He doesn't go talk to the devil about you! When we biblically confront "trespassers," as we are told to, we get clarity over what happened and we can navigate beyond the offense. Many times, the situation is not what it seems to be.

A Painful Conversation

Years ago, I was in what we call a watch night service, which is simply a New Year's Eve service. In our church we would praise and worship on New Year's Eve, and right before the New Year began, we would wash one another's feet. Our pastor took the opportunity to encourage us to forgive those we had offenses toward—and then take the next step and wash their feet in particular.

On this night, a person came immediately to my mind. It was an older brother in the church who was very opinionated and outspoken and seemed to always have something cynical and negative to say to me. For instance, if someone congratulated me on being accepted into school, he would come along and say, "That school is too expensive and you probably won't make any money with that degree anyway!" If I had an idea of how to build up our church, he would shoot it down with a bit of sarcasm. I regularly felt demeaned by him, and after this had gone on for some time, I was very offended!

So when the pastor asked us to reconcile with the people who offended us, I instantly thought of this brother. Well, he just so happened to be in attendance. So in obedience to my pastor's instruction, I went to him. I said, "Brother, I need to talk to you." I told him that I was offended with him. I told him that it was a matter of a difference in our personalities. But as I was speaking, he suddenly interrupted me. "No, let me stop you there! This is not a matter of a difference in personality. You realized that I was jealous of you. And I have to be honest. Not only am I jealous of you, but I know many other brothers in this church who are jealous of you as well." He then apologized for harboring negative feelings about me.

I was taken aback! Here I was focusing on one aspect of the offense, not realizing that it went much deeper than just what I was experiencing. This is why Jesus commands us to go directly to our brother: it gives us the opportunity to resolve the situation and bring clarity.

In contrast, anytime we choose to go to a third party instead of going directly to our brother or sister, we leave the situation unresolved, and unresolved conflict is the root of bitterness and offense. Of course, we must do it in a spirit of love and humility, not anger and frustration. And we must seek reconciliation, not a vindication of our opinion!

SATAN'S LIE:
IF SOMEONE'S HURT YOU,
AVOID THEM.
#AMOREEXCELLENTWAY

Even so, many situations are too serious to be so resolved and must involve a third party. But what I'm trying to say is that we have to put first things first! When we truly seek to find common ground and go directly to our brother or sister *first* before involving others, we will find that most of our offenses will be resolved. Or we will find the underlying root—like I did with the brothers in my church—and be able to understand what's really going on.

A Better Way to Respond

One day, while ministering overseas, I had the opportunity to sit down with an older couple that was in desperate need of God's intervention and restoration. They had been estranged from their local church for several months and wanted me to minister to them. As we began to talk, I could sense that their pain ran very deep within their hearts. I asked them what happened.

It all started, they said, over some clothing that they wanted to sell to the church to get some extra money for outstanding bills. Apparently, there was a miscommunication about the clothing being given to the church, and the church received them as a donation instead of a sale. This couple never received any money in exchange for their clothing. In the midst of their distress over not being able to meet some pertinent financial obligations, they attempted to either collect money for the clothing or get the items returned to them. But another church member who was actively involved in this situation made some insensitive and offensive remarks to this couple. They never received the money they were expecting and, on top of it, felt humiliated by someone in leadership. They were so hurt by this experience that they left the church and hadn't been back since.

WHEN WE AVOID THE PERSON WHO OFFENDED US AND OPT FOR A THIRD-PARTY, WE ARE LESS LIKELY GET TO THE ROOT OF THE PROBLEM.

This couple asked me for advice. The first thing I told them to do was to go and talk with their pastor.

"Why should we have to go to him?" she asked.

"Because the Bible tells you to!" I exclaimed.

The couple looked at me with a bit of shock. Apparently, the senior pastor was not even aware that any of this had transpired; the situation never even made it to his desk. Contrary to popular opinion, pastors are not mind-readers! There are many things that are never even brought to a pastor's attention—as a pastor, I can attest to that myself!

Many people think that when they joined the church that they joined heaven. Nothing could be further from the truth.

And when people find out that church members do indeed offend, they turn around and leave. This couple never considered that they were responsible to actually speak to the people who offended them. Yet this is exactly what the Bible tells us to do:

Moreover if your brother shall trespass against you, go and tell him his fault between you and him alone: if he shall hear you, you have gained your brother. But if he will not hear you, then take with you one or two more, that in the mouth of two or three witnesses every word may be established. And if he shall neglect to hear them, tell it to the church: but if he neglect to hear the church, let him be to you as a heathen man and a publican. (Matthew 18:15–17)

SATAN'S LIE:
WHEN YOU JOIN A CHURCH,
IT WILL BE PERFECT.
#AMOREEXCELLENTWAY

This couple did not obey the biblical mandate to go to the one who hurt them. Instead, they chose to accuse their brother. Can you imagine how many people they called and discussed this matter with before it came to me? Tragically, not one of those discussions was with the pastor of the church. This is not the Spirit of God! As a result of their offense, this couple was embittered and in bondage. In fact, their bodies were suffering from arthritis and other debilitating illnesses. I believe the only one who stood to gain from this situation was Satan himself. He was the one spewing accusations against that church and against that pastor in the hearts and minds of this precious couple. Though their pain felt legitimate, it was keeping them from enjoying the blessings of God. As we prayed and cried, they began to experience healing. God's Word provides us with the blueprint for having successful relationships and living out the abundant life. When we fail to obey God's Word, we do so at the cost of our own peace and freedom.

Motives Matter!

I have to be honest with you; this is a very personal subject for me. I have battled with bitterness and offense in my own life in the past, before the Lord eventually liberated me from their destructive hold. The irony was, I didn't even know I was offended. You see it is very easy for us to look at *others* as the ones at fault. It is easy for us to shift the blame to someone else, because we can physically see him or her. I never realized that Satan was masking himself behind my pain, hurt, and disappointment, and manipulating me into focusing my attention on what others were doing to me, and my right to be offended, rather than seeing him for the liar and deceiver he really is.

I have learned throughout the years to never go to the devil for information. He will lie every time! And no, I don't mean that he sits on your front porch wearing a cobra suit and hissing in your ear. It would be easy to call the cops on that! But just as he was subtle with Eve, he is subtle with us. He works through the voices of gossip, slander, and false accusation. When we listen to them, we are listening to the devil.

IT IS THE NATURE OF THE ENEMY TO ACCUSE AND SLANDER, BUT IT IS THE NATURE OF CHRIST TO LOVE AND COVER.

You must understand that the devil witnessed the creation of man, a perfect being created in the very image of God Almighty. He was present when God made a species that would be more celebrated than Satan. The devil was jealous of humankind and wanted more than anything else to see them displaced from the garden. His motives were always to steal, kill, and destroy. By definition, slander means a malicious intent to demean, denigrate, and cast a shadow over the victim. Unfortunately, Eve never questioned the motive of the Serpent even though motives are the most important aspect of any conversation. Always ask, "What's your motive?" Remember that slander not only involves a negative accusation, but also *intent* to defame.

Often people bring frustrations and accusations to me, as the pastor, expecting me to come to a conclusion about the accused. Many times, the accuser seems very sincere and genuine. However, I've come to realize that there are always *three* sides to every story—our side, their side, and the truth.

I can remember a person bringing an accusation about someone in the church to me. They quoted Scripture. They looked me in the eye with distress and victimhood. Clearly they were the mature, biblically balanced, super-spiritual saint who had been done wrong. Right? Wrong!

Upon meeting with these individuals in private, I quickly realized that things were not necessarily the way they were initially portrayed to me. Come to find out, there was much more to the story than I was told. The real offense had nothing to do with the accusation, but with something much more trivial. It basically boiled down to, "Pastor, I didn't like the way they spoke to me!" This matter should have been sorted out between the two individuals by themselves. It was unnecessary for me to get involved, but the offended party wanted vindication for the hurt they experienced—even to the point of exaggerating a story.

I learned a very valuable lesson that day: things are not always as they seem! Now, I often tell people to sort out their problems with the other person first before they involve me. Why do I approach things this way? I don't want to be an accomplice in someone's attempt to slander another person. Don't get me wrong; everyone is not attempting to slander another person when they report a problem or a concern. The litmus test is always, *what's the motive?*

What was the devil's motive in the garden that day? He was attempting to discredit God and ruin the chances Adam and Eve had of ruling and reigning in the earth. Thank God we serve a merciful and loving Creator who had a plan of redemption before man was even created. Hallelujah! As it says in Proverbs, *"A man's heart devises his way: but the* LORD *directs his steps"* (16:9).

Developing a Defense Against Offense

We must learn to develop a defense against offense. When I was a kid, we had what we called the five-second rule. Maybe you had something similar. The upshot was that if you dropped food on the floor but picked it up before five seconds transpired, you could still eat it without fear of contamination. Of course, the five-second rule is kind of ridiculous and has no basis in scientific fact or evidence. The truth is that the food was just as dirty in one second as it was in five seconds. However, the point of this rule was to create a buffer or a time space in which we made allowance for ourselves to eat the food, even though it fell to the ground.

The same five-second concept can help us create a defense against offense. We must have an internal buffer that prevents us from immediately accepting an offense into our mind or heart. Before you allow your mind to go down the dark road of taking offense, ask yourself, "Is this really worth it?" Take five seconds to consider the consequences before consuming the offense into your heart. Offense is like raw sewage: once you walk in it, it leaves a very nasty residue that can be a challenge to remove. It is better to avoid it! Can you imagine raw sewage flooding your home? God forbid! Yet there are thousands if not millions of believers who accept bitterness in their lives. Too many Christians are allowing themselves to be contaminated by the sewage of offense. They do not realize its damaging effects. Yes, it may gratify your pride in the short run, but in the long run, you will be the one who suffers the most.

SATAN'S LIE:
BEING OFFENDED JUST MEANS
YOU'RE STICKING UP FOR YOURSELF.
#AMOREEXCELLENTWAY

There are three things you must resolve in your mind if you want to develop a defense against offense:

1. I will not *be* offended.

2. My spiritual condition is more important than my pain.

3. I will not *stay* offended.

Once you resolve in your heart and mind that you will not be offended, it will become much more difficult for offenses to attach themselves to your thought life. You must never underestimate the power of a made-up mind. When you have decided that you will not allow the actions of others to manipulate or control you, you will be empowered to make quality, biblically based decisions. After you have made up your mind to not be offended, you must resolve that your spiritual well-being is more important than your alleged "right to be offended." This will cause you to cross-examine and interrogate your thoughts. Is it really worth it? I know that you may be feeling the pain or disappointment, but is it worth your joy and your peace of mind? If you have already opened the door to offense in your life, you must now make the decision to not *stay* offended.

You are probably thinking to yourself, *How can I choose not to be offended?* Is that even a realistic concept? The truth is, there are many situations and circumstances that are beyond our control. You couldn't help the circumstances surrounding your birth. You couldn't help the fact that your parents got a divorce. You couldn't even control the situations that transpired in your church before you arrived. However, we do have the power to control our response to these things. Whether an offense is justifiable is really irrelevant, because *staying offended* is never acceptable and is strictly forbidden by Scripture. God's requirement to love and forgive is not based on convenience. Even when reconciliation is not possible, we should endeavor to live in peace with others and ourselves.

WE MUST MAKE THE DECISION TO LIVE FREE FROM OFFENSE ALL OVER AGAIN EVERY SINGLE DAY OF OUR LIVES.

Faith Versus Feelings

One of the problems in our modern culture is that we have been taught to live by our feelings. We believe that if we feel something, it automatically legitimizes the subsequent actions connected to our feelings. However, the Bible tells us not to trust our hearts! *"The heart is deceitful above all things, and desperately wicked: who can know it?"* (Jeremiah 17:9). Contrary to popular culture, what you feel (or what is in your heart) is not always legitimate, especially if it is not based on the Word of God. We must learn to subject what we feel to God's truth. You may not *feel* like going to work in the morning, but your bills still need to be paid. The same is true spiritually. Instead of asking yourself, *how do I feel about this?* ask *what does God's Word say about this?*

One time a woman came to me saying that she felt that the Lord was leading her to separate from her husband. I asked, "Do you have biblical reason for divorce? Are there problems and issues with him?" and she replied, "No, I just feel in my spirit that I'm supposed to leave him."

I can't tell you the countless times people have "felt" their way into chaos and confusion. Whether we like it or not, God makes the rules and we must follow them. Remember that His wisdom spans all ages—and in fact created the whole world in the first place! Our minds, on the contrary, are all too often limited to this age and what the people around us are saying and thinking. We are usually the ones bringing the spirit of the age into the church, and it usually isn't healthy.

I don't know about you, but there have been countless times when I chose to follow my feelings instead of following what I knew God told me to do. It always ended badly. Now, I'm not saying that feelings aren't important, because they absolutely are! God often uses them to point us in the right direction or to affirm and strengthen our relationships and decisions. However, we must keep them in the proper context. How we feel about something should never replace what God says about something. The Holy Spirit will never instruct you to do something that goes against the Word of God.

This issue of feeling is especially prevalent in the Western church. It is a luxury of a more affluent culture. Instead of being faced with basic needs every morning (where will I sleep tonight? How will I feed my kids? How will I pay the heating bill?), many of us are faced with a huge array of choices (Which toothpaste should I use? Which deli meat should I have for lunch? Which shoes go with these pants?). And we've been taught to trust our feelings in order to make the decision between all these choices. Think about it. How many ads are designed simply to prey upon our feelings and desires, thereby influencing our decisions? Old Spice. McDonald's. Apple. They all seek to manipulate our emotions!

IF IT WASN'T WHAT GOD SAID,
YOU CAN BE SURE IT WASN'T WHAT GOD LED.

It is a part of the psychobabble culture that we have embraced here in the Western world. We are encouraged to be in touch with our emotions at all times. Parents even ask permission from their little children before they take action—"How do you *feel* about going to Grandma's tonight?"

Now, like I mentioned earlier, I grew up in a very legalistic culture. There was right, and there was wrong, and woe woe woe on anyone who does wrong. That culture is unhealthy because there is no room for grace, but only law. But let's not swing to the opposite extreme and get rid of law altogether! What did Jesus say? "I come not to abolish the law but to fulfill it." (See Matthew 5:17.) The law is still here. Jesus lived a perfect life and fulfilled the law's requirements so that we don't *earn* our salvation; it comes by *grace*. Yet, how should we respond to that grace? By following the Word out of gratitude!

> *What shall we say then? Are we to continue in sin that grace may abound? By no means!… Let not sin therefore reign in your mortal body, to make you obey its passions. Do not present your members to sin as instruments for unrighteousness, but present yourselves to God as those who have been brought from death to life, and your members to God as instruments for righteousness. For sin will have no dominion over you, since you are not under law but under grace.*
> (Romans 6:1–2, 12–14 ESV)

What are those passions that we so easily obey? In today's language, we'd call them feelings.

We often run from things we don't like and don't want to do. We run from biblical confrontation because it would call us to communicate the things that have hurt or wounded us. If we do that, we are accountable for our negative feelings. And quite frankly people don't like accountability. Take this as your verse to help wade through the feelings: "sin shall no longer have dominion over me!" (See Romans 6:14).

As Christ Prayed

In addition to emotionalizing our decisions, we tend to spiritualize them as well. When someone is making a wrong decision, they often use spirituality to justify themselves. Once I asked a person why they didn't follow the biblical requirement found in Matthew 18 to go directly to the person who offended them. They responded that they just didn't feel the need in their spirit. Ironically, Jesus didn't "feel" the need in His Spirit to suffer and die for our sins. He prayed to the Father in the garden, *"If You be willing, remove this cup from Me: nevertheless not My will, but Yours, be done"* (Luke 22:42). What a beautiful prayer! And I am so happy that even though He prayed that the cup be removed, when it wasn't, He still drank it to the last bitter drop because He knew that's what the will of the Father was.

When we don't feel the need in our hearts to do something, we can honestly pray, "Father, take this from me!" And if He doesn't take it away, we have to drink it. You can pray. But don't make excuses for disobeying the highest Being in the universe.

For Discussion

1. According to Matthew 18:15–17, what should you do if you are offended by a sister or a brother? Have you ever done this?

2. What are the three things to resolve in your mind to develop a defense against offense?

3. Does the Bible says it's wrong to feel emotion—joy, love, anger, frustration, etc.? When are emotions problematic?

Testimony

I was terrified of conflict and confrontation, and had been that way my entire life. For me, confrontation represented negativity, and I believed that there was always a winner and a loser in situations like that. So I chose to avoid confronting *anybody*, even at the expense of my own peace of mind and with the possibility of missing out on quality relationships with people I knew I wanted and needed in my life.

One night at church, the pastor was speaking about boundaries and conflict, and one of the major points of the message was that where the boundaries of valuing the person, honoring them, and examining my own motives and are put in place, there is no need or room for fear of conflict or confrontation. Basically, if I truly loved and valued my friend and made that known before addressing the issue, then everything would be and would remain ok. No matter what. I made the decision to live my life with that assurance from that night forward.

Before we dismissed that night, the pastor asked us to do a practical exercise in which we picked a partner and "confronted" them, and I linked up with the person behind me. He had to make up a situation to do the exercise, but I didn't! I was at that moment struggling with whether or not to confront someone I cared about a whole lot, and practicing what I learned that night—to express what I was feeling in a healthy way—opened my eyes to the benefits of godly confrontation. I hadn't even spoken to the actual person yet but just knowing that I could approach the situation correctly and gently, and that everything would be fine because of the high level of value I placed on my friend, made me eager to restore our relationship immediately. And I did just that. Nothing can compare to real freedom, which always comes from handling things the way God teaches us to handle them.

—*Anonymous*

Prayer

Father, in the name of Jesus, I thank You for who You are and all that You have done in my life. Father, I recognize that offense is a spirit that does not come from You. I take authority over the spirit of offense and command it to leave every area of my life. I refuse to operate in a spirit of offense. I freely forgive all those who have offended, hurt, or wounded me. I break the power of offense off of my life and the lives of my loved ones. I recognize that my kingdom assignment is more important than offense. I cast down every vain imagination and demolish every mental stronghold. Every negative thought must leave me now. I will live free from all bondage in my life. In the name of Jesus.

Amen.

8
BEWARE OF BALAAM
AND ABSALOM

And God said to Balaam, You shall not go with them; you shall not curse the people: for they are blessed. (Numbers 22:12)

I want to share with you a very interesting and profound story from the Bible. It features a peculiar prophet by the name of Balaam. Listen to what happened:

And the children of Israel set forward, and pitched in the plains of Moab on this side Jordan by Jericho.

And Balak the son of Zippor saw all that Israel had done to the Amorites.

And Moab was sore afraid of the people, because they were many: and Moab was distressed because of the children of Israel.

And Moab said unto the elders of Midian, Now shall this company lick up all that are round about us, as the ox licks up the grass of the field. And Balak the son of Zippor was king of the Moabites at that time.

He sent messengers therefore to Balaam the son of Beor to Pethor, which is by the river of the land of the children of his people, to call him, saying, Behold, there is a people come out from Egypt: behold, they cover the face of the earth, and they abide opposite me:

Come now therefore, I pray you, curse me this people; for they are too mighty for me: perhaps I shall prevail, that we may smite them, and that I may drive them out of the land: for I know that he whom you bless is blessed, and he whom you curse is cursed.

And the elders of Moab and the elders of Midian departed with the rewards of divination in their hand; and they came unto Balaam, and spoke to him the words of Balak.

And he said to them, Lodge here this night, and I will bring you word again, as the LORD shall speak to me: and the princes of Moab abode with Balaam.

And God came to Balaam, and said, What men are these with you?

And Balaam said to God, Balak the son of Zippor, king of Moab, has sent to me, saying, Behold, there is a people come out of Egypt, which covers the face of the earth: come now, curse me them; perhaps I shall be able to overcome them, and drive them out.

And God said to Balaam, You shall not go with them; you shall not curse the people: for they are blessed.   (Numbers 22:1–12)

The Moabite king, Balak, heard about the dreadful works of the Israelites, and was afraid that they would take over his kingdom. So he offered the prophet Balaam money to pronounce a curse over the children of Israel. But God told Balaam that he could not, for the children of Israel were blessed.

Balaam and Today's Believer

What does this story have to do with our conversation about slander, gossip, and offense? What if I told you that slander was much more than just speaking negative or damaging statements about someone else? What if I told you that engaging in these activities actually fell under the category of "cursing" others?

We should probably stop here and define what I mean by "curse." The term "curse" here refers to an execration or a solemn utterance, intended to invoke a supernatural power to inflict harm or punishment on someone or something. In other words, a curse is an imprecation of evil.

Essentially, Balak was asking Baalam to use his words and his influence to speak evil over Israel, thus causing them to be destroyed. Praise God, the Bible says that whom God has blessed, no man can curse! (See Numbers 23:8.)

The same clandestine and sinister scheme is being executed in the church today. But the Bible tells us, *"Bless them which persecute you: bless, and curse not"* (Romans 12:14). If the Bible tells us to bless and curse not, it certainly suggests that even Christians are capable of cursing others. And indeed, scores of believers are using their mouths to speak evil of their fellow brothers and sisters in Christ.

SATAN'S LIE: CHRISTIANS CAN'T CURSE EACH OTHER.

#BEWAREOFBALAAM

One day I was on the phone with a pastor, and this guy began to tell me how he had heard from the Lord that several churches in our city were going to be exposed. The pastor told me that God had marked these churches for destruction. He went further to say that he had pronounced judgment on these churches. When he made this statement something inside of me cringed. This just did not seem like the Holy Spirit at all! I do not believe that this was the will of God! And I am totally convinced that this goes against Scripture. Whether this pastor knew it or not, he was speaking a curse over those churches. He was using his tongue to pronounce calamity and destruction over God's church. Unfortunately, one of the churches he mentioned was eventually dismantled. What would have been the outcome had this pastor blessed the church rather than cursed it?

The Dangers of a Judging Spirit

I've often heard people say that it is our job to expose sin in each other. They feel that we must speak against people and things that are wrong. I disagree! While I am all for speaking the truth boldly and standing up for holiness, that is very different from singling people out for their errors and announcing an imprecation. There is no Scripture in the Bible that tells us to go around exposing everybody's sins. But there *are* Scriptures in the Bible that tell us to examine ourselves. (See, for example, Psalm 119:59; Lamentations 3:40; Matthew 7:5; 1 Corinthians 11:27–31; Galatians 6:4; 1 John 3:20–21.)

GOD HAS CALLED US TO SPEAK BLESSINGS, NOT CURSES, OVER FAMILIES, MINISTRIES, AND OURSELVES.

I can speak on this subject because I was guilty of the very thing I'm denouncing. For years I made it my business to identify and call out the sins of others, not realizing that God wanted me to address sin in my own life first.

Many people feel that if they bless instead of curse, they are just being weak. According to human eyesight, the toughest, biggest, loudest, meanest person is also the strongest. Nothing could be further than the truth! According to the story of the little nation of Israel and the words of Jesus Himself, the truth is that whoever knows his or her weakness will be made strong. Consider these verses:

A little one shall become a thousand, and a small one a strong nation: I the LORD will hasten it in his time. (Isaiah 60:22)

Because the foolishness of God is wiser than men; and the weakness of God is stronger than men. (1 Corinthians 1:25)

And He said to me, My grace is sufficient for you: for My strength is made perfect in weakness. Most gladly therefore will I rather glory in my infirmities, that the power of Christ may rest upon me. (2 Corinthians 12:9)

Jesus, when He was hanging on the cross, did not take that opportunity to call down fire and judgment on His persecutors, but instead prayed, *"Father, forgive them; for they know not what they do"* (Luke 23:34). Surely He should have cursed the high priest, Judas Iscariot who sold him for thirty pieces of silver, or even His own disciples for deserting Him in His darkest hour; but instead we see something totally different from our Lord. He *blessed* the very people who were doing evil toward Him. Can you believe this? We must follow in His footsteps! We are to pray for our enemies and do good to those who spitefully use us and persecute us. (See Matthew 5:44.)

Have you ever experienced pain or heartache at the hands of another? I went through a painful experience some years ago, when someone who was very close to me hurt me in a very deep way. To add insult to injury, this person went about slandering me and speaking things against me, most of which were not true. I wanted to defend myself and clear my name! But one day, while crafting a well-thought-out defense against the slander, the Holy Spirit spoke to me in a very clear and concise way. He said to me, "Don't say a word." I was dumbfounded at this instruction. "But God, don't you know they are speaking against me? They are dishonoring the man of God!" I insisted. But again I heard the still, small voice: "Don't say a word." Then the Lord went on to say, "Bless them." With tears in my eyes and a heart full of pain, I began to speak blessings over this person.

EVERY TIME WE SPEAK IN DEFENSE OF OURSELVES, WE HINDER THE RIGHTEOUS JUDGMENT OF GOD FROM COMING FORTH. SPEAK FACTS, BUT LEAVE THE DEFENSE TO THE MOST HIGH!

It's tempting to want to set the record straight. But God's Word tells us to bless those who offend us. By blessing the person who hurt me, I was releasing myself from bondage. All of a sudden, I began to experience a freedom that I had never experienced before. My heart became lighter, my mind became clearer, and I could praise God without the debilitating pain of offense in my heart.

The point of my testimony is not to pretend that I have never wronged anyone, nor even to suggest that I didn't hurt the person that I just spoke about. The point is that relationships can be extremely challenging and even people with the best intentions step on other people's toes. But judging whoever has done the wrong and defending ourselves doesn't help the situation. True power is found in submitting ourselves to the situation, to God, and to blessing others rather than participating in self-righteous cursing.

Witchcraft in the Church

In the story of Balaam, the Moabite king represents Satan. Satan, like Balak, does not have the power to curse the children of God himself, so he uses people within the church to do his bidding. Anytime we use our mouth to pronounce evil over another person, we are in fact releasing a curse over them, and participating in a spirit of witchcraft.

As a child, the concept of witchcraft never really made much sense to me. Honestly, I thought it only existed in cartoons. However, as I grew older and began to travel the world preaching the gospel, I came to experience the power of the dark side firsthand. I have witnessed people manifest demonically right before my very eyes.

Maybe you have a similar concept of witchcraft as I used to. You may be envisioning an African witchdoctor or a Haitian voodoo priest. However, the American church has some of the most extreme forms of witchcraft I have ever witnessed in all my travels. I am not talking about séances or astral projection: I am talking about the witchcraft that flows from the pews and often from the pulpit.

In Galatians 5:19–21, it reads: *"Now the works of the flesh are manifest, which are these; adultery, fornication, uncleanness, lasciviousness, idolatry, witchcraft, hatred, variance, emulations, wrath, strife, seditions, heresies, envyings, murders, drunkenness, revellings, and such like: of the which I tell you before, as I have also told you in time past, that they which do such things shall not inherit the kingdom of God."* Here we see a listing of the *"works of the flesh"* and listed among them is *"witchcraft."* This word comes from the Greek *pharmakeia*, which is translated: the use or the administration of drugs, poisoning, or sorcery, magical arts, and deception.

Why would the Bible warn us against witchcraft? Wasn't the apostle Paul writing to Christians? There is much more to this concept than we often realize. This word is where we get the word *pharmacy*. In other words, Paul is referring to those "pharmacists" in the church who poison people with their words. There are many spiritual pharmacists that are dealing illegal prescriptions in the church—not narcotics or oxycodone, but slander and false accusations. Their price is cheap but the cost is tremendous. They are in fact a form of manipulation and control that the Bible calls *"witchcraft."* The Word of God forbids this!

ANY TIME A PERSON USES THEIR WORDS TO IMPLORE EVIL, PAIN, DESTRUCTION, OR CALAMITY IN THE LIFE OF ANOTHER, THEY ARE PRACTICING WITCHCRAFT.

People sometimes make the assumption that when we speak of witchcraft in the church we are exaggerating, but we are not! There are many churches full of parishioners practicing witchcraft in the pews. Some of them are aware of it and some are not.

There are two extremes when it comes to witchcraft: manipulation and control as a work of the flesh, and sorcery. Sorcery involves employing the power of evil spirits to inflict harm on another person either spiritually or physically. Many people do not start out with the intention of employing evil spirits, they are simply wounded and frustrated. But if there is no repentance of this behavior, it will eventually progress into sorcery. If witchcraft is manipulation and control, then those who practice this ungodly activity are witches and warlocks.

I heard a story of a pastor who was frustrated at the slow growth of his ministry. He prayed and fasted, wondering why the church was not progressing. The worship was amazing. The Word was powerful. What was the problem? As he fasted and prayed, the Lord began to uncover witchcraft in the church. One of the core leaders in the church was poisoning the people in an attempt to usurp the authority of the pastor. On another occasion, I heard about an intercessory leader who was releasing curses over key leaders in the congregation, and as she did, they began to fall ill—one by one. Finally, the people in the church realized what was going on and took authority over this satanic activity and removed this person from leadership.

The Spirit of Absalom

Do you know the biblical story of a man named Absalom, the third son of King David? Absalom got himself into a world of hurt, and it all began with an almost unthinkable crime. Another son of David, Amnon, had an incestuous attraction to his own sister, Tamar, and raped her. It is difficult to imagine something so perverse. King David heard of this tragic situation, yet he did not punish his son Amnon.

Absalom was enraged that his sister, Tamar, had not received justice! Two years later, Absalom resolved to take it into his own hands and kill his brother Amnon—and he did. To flee his father's retribution for the murder, Absalom fled the country. Years later, he finally returned to Jerusalem to yet again take matters into his own hands:

> And Absalom rose up early, and stood beside the way of the gate: and it was so, that when any man that had a controversy came to the king for judgment, then Absalom called to him, and said, Of what city are you? And he said, Your servant is of one of the tribes of Israel. And Absalom said to him, See, your matters are good and right; but there is no man deputed of the king to hear you. Absalom said moreover, Oh that I were made judge in the land, that every man which has any suit or cause might come to me, and I would do him justice!
>
> (2 Samuel 15:2–4)

Notice a couple of things about this biblical account. Absalom was enraged at his brother Amnon—because Amnon did indeed do a terrible thing. But Absalom let that rage turn into bitterness over the course of years, until he took the law in his own hands and killed Amnon. We can certainly understand his anger, but Absalom did not deal with the anger well. Why did he not immediately insist that King David execute justice?

Then, when Absalom was in exile, instead of moving on with his life, it would appear that he let his bitterness against his father fester and grow into a huge scheme to overthrow his father and take over the kingdom. The scheme was to convince everyone that he would actually be a better king than his father and to sow discord and discontent over his father's rule. And sure enough, the Bible records, *"Absalom stole the hearts of the men of Israel"* (2 Samuel 15:6).

Oftentimes, when people hear the story of Absalom, they focus on the fact that he supplanted the kingdom of his father. They focus on the rebellion that divided the kingdom of Israel and led to his own destruction. But I think the focus should be on the *heart* of Absalom, because it was the offense in Absalom's heart that motivated him to poison the minds of the people of Israel against his father.

The Absalom Syndrome

Absalom is a perfect picture of witchcraft in the church. He spoke against his father. He slandered his father's name. Can you imagine speaking against the king of Israel? Witches in the church speak against leadership under the guise of superior spirituality. They say, "The pastor really needs to hear from God!" They often do this in an attempt to undermine the leadership and to paint him or her in a negative light.

I can remember a particular instance when a man in a church I was attending pulled me to the side and said that the pastor was not hearing from God. He said we needed to pray for the pastor to really get a revelation from the Holy Spirit. He ultimately left the church, but I never forgot the experience. Why couldn't he pray for the pastor himself? Why couldn't he go to the pastor directly? Why involve me? The reason why this gentleman said those things is because he was offended with the pastor. He had a personal grievance that he wanted to spread to others. This is very dangerous! Like Absalom's heart, the motives of his heart were impure. It is one thing for us to be hurt; it is another for us to spread the hurt to other people. Once we open our mouths and speak against a leader, we are engaging in slander for which God will hold us accountable.

BE CAREFUL OF PEOPLE WHO ALWAYS TALK ABOUT PROBLEMS BUT WHO NEVER BRING SOLUTIONS.

Unfortunately, there are so many people who spew accusations, criticism, and other forms of slander out of their mouths with the effect of poisoning the listeners. I often speak to people who attend churches in which the pastor has deeply wounded or hurt them. These individuals have nothing good to say about their pastor. I ask them, "Why would you stay in a church where you don't trust or respect the pastor?" Their reply is, "God has not released me!" Friend, if you are at a place where you find yourself spreading negativity about leadership, you need to leave the situation! You are released! Don't become an Absalom!

The story that I just shared with you is an example of what I call the "Absalom Syndrome." People who are suffering from this syndrome have a tendency to draw people to themselves for the wrong reasons. They are often seeking the wrong kind of validation from others. Their hurt has caused them to take on a mind-set that is divisive and destructive. Absalom acted out of his pain and killed his own brother, and this is the same behavior exemplified by "spiritual Absaloms"; they kill others—who may or may not be acting uprightly—with slander and gossip. Instead of fostering peace and unity, they facilitate strife, division, and wounding in the body of Christ.

Word Curses

Earlier, we introduced the concept of "word curses." These are words spoken against another person with the intent of harming or negatively affecting them. Word curses also fall under the category of witchcraft. In fact, we often refer to this practice as charismatic or evangelical witchcraft because it is so prevalent in charismatic and evangelical churches.

SATAN'S LIE:
AS LONG AS YOU LOVE JESUS,
YOU CAN SAY WHAT YOU WANT.
#BEWAREOFBALAAM

Someone told me a story about a pastor with one son. This son desired to move to another country and build a business. Of course the pastor was not in agreement with her son moving to another country and so she began to pray against it. The son moved anyway. The mother began to pray that all of his business ventures would fail and that nothing he touched would prosper. Interestingly enough, all his ventures crumbled and he ultimately came back to his home to live with his mother. This is another example of someone using their prayers to control the will of someone else. This is not acceptable.

Please do not misunderstand me. I am all for speaking the truth, but it is wrong to do so with malicious intent. The Bible commands us to speak the truth in love. Truth without love is abuse. And love without truth is deception.[2] When we correct a person or bring rebuke, we must

2. A variation of Warren Wiersbe's "Truth without love is brutality, and love without truth is hypocrisy."

keep in mind that God's intent is to heal, deliver, and restore that person to wholeness. If restoration is not at the root of all words and actions, then we have greatly missed the mark. I pray that God will reveal His heart to us so that we can become true ministers of reconciliation.

The Heart Connection

There is a direct connection between the condition of our heart and our ability to receive and walk in the favor and blessings of God in our lives. The apostle John tells us that we will prosper in proportion to our internal prosperity, or in other words, in proportion to the condition of our soul: *"Beloved, I wish above all things that you may prosper and be in health, even as your soul prospers"* (3 John 2). In fact, I have found that most times when I am tempted to be hurt or offended, there is always a harvest to reap on the other side when I refuse to be offended. Too many pastors, leaders, churchgoers, and employees are experiencing lack, stagnation, and even sickness as a result of bitterness and offense. This is what I call the heart connection.

ANYTIME WE SPEAK EVIL OF ANOTHER PERSON,
WITH NEGATIVE INTENTIONS,
WE ARE IN FACT RELEASING A CURSE OVER THEM.

Most trials and tribulations that we go through are a spiritual battle over the territory of our hearts. Are you winning or losing this battle? What is the condition of your heart? Are you walking in love and forgiveness? If not, Satan is robbing you of your peace and prosperity. Don't jeopardize your breakthrough, healing, and harvest for the temporary gratification that offense seems to bring. Let go and let God!

For Discussion

1. Have you ever felt used by the devil like Balaam was used by Balak? Describe.

2. What mistakes did Absalom make in dealing with his brother's terrible crime?

3. Where can we find witchcraft in the church?

Practicum

1. Were you recently offended by a brother or sister? Pray through Matthew 18:15–17, and (if it is a non-threatening situation) arrange for a time to meet with them to share your hurt. Pray for a forgiving heart of humility and love.

2. It is when we are weak that we are strong. Are their areas in your life where you are trying to be the strong one instead of handing it over to God? Pray through 2 Corinthians 12:9, asking for God's strength, not human strength.

3. The chapter mentions one kind of word curse: using prayer to control the actions of others. What other word curses do Christians participate in?

Testimony

When I got saved in 2012, the Lord spoke to me regarding my calling and said that the next several years would be on-the-job training. The Lord quickly showed me that dying to the flesh daily is a must, and to do so, I must give myself completely to Him. Immediately after I was saved, I was placed into leadership and became the pastor's assistant. Over the next three years, I learned that we must become the walking, living Christ.

But I became so intertwined with becoming a leader that I placed it before my family and even before my relationship with God. In doing so, every burden that my pastor carried fell on my shoulders.

I quickly began to fall away from seeking God because my eyes and heart were on man. Holding myself alone accountable for my faith and life, I never spoke about it or reached out for help. You see, many times leaders think they cannot have any problems, trials, or tribulations. When I looked at the other leaders and pastors, they were all too busy focusing on bringing new members into church and raising funds to give me help or guidance. My hope and faith were slowly dying out. The outer self looked alive, but the inner was dead.

By 2015, things were so desperate and my depression so intense that I attempted to take my own life. I did not succeed, was rushed to the hospital, and was placed on life support—still alive but not likely to ever wake up. The toxicity level inside my body was so high, there was no earthly way I could ever come out of my coma.

But as my body lay lifeless, Jesus Himself showed up. In my right ear, I heard the demons calling for my soul, and in my left ear I heard the voice of compassion, love, and life. He explained that the reason I was unable to love His people the way He loved them was because of the condition of my heart. He proceeded to do a heart transplant and give me His. He rooted His Word in my heart, and reminded me that I now live only for Him. I have learned that He is my Life, Comforter, Provider, Deliverer, Counselor, Healer, and it is He that I seek for all revelation, guidance, wisdom, and knowledge. He healed my body from major depression, anxiety, bipolar, borderline personality disorder, PTSD, fibromyalgia, sciatica, rheumatoid arthritis, osteoarthritis, and degenerative discs. I was taking twenty-five medications as well as extensive Electrical Shock Treatment. When He sent me back, I was completely transformed. Faith is key! It is the key to kingdom authority. Through this, God has restored my health, marriage, family, and now I have been sent forth to be a walking testimony to bring healing and deliverance to those who suffer with mental illness.

This is only a brief description of what happened, but this is the most important part: through it, Jesus showed me that *I* am the church, His holy temple, and through my faith in Him, life more abundantly has been promised! Through this miraculous encounter with my heavenly Father, heaven has come to me here on earth, and through my faith in Him all things are possible! Maximum obedience and maximum faith! —*Liz*

Prayer

Lord, Your Word has revealed that my tongue can be a weapon or it could be an instrument of healing. Today I choose to use my tongue as an instrument of healing. I will never curse God's people nor will I curse myself. Thank You, Lord, for Your grace and mercy in this area of my life. Forgive me for speaking things that violate Your Word. I ask that You forgive me for having negative thoughts and feelings toward my brothers and sisters in Christ. From this day forward, I make the decision to operate in grace. I cancel every word curse that I have spoken out of my mouth or even thought in my mind. I choose to walk in Your love and in Your truth, in the name of Jesus.

Amen!

9
THE ASSASSIN'S CREED

Whosoever hates his brother is a murderer: and you know that no murderer has eternal life abiding in him. (1 John 3:15)

The Bible tells us plainly, *"Whosoever hates his brother is a murderer."* These are very strong words! Why would the Bible equate hating someone with committing the act of murder? What is meant by the term *murderer?* The Greek word here is *anthrōpoktonos*, which means *manslayer* or *assassin*. Whoever walks in hatred toward their brother or sister is a manslayer, an assassin. Now, if you've watched any movies at all, you'll know that assassins are always working for somebody else—who usually doesn't want to be known. If the Bible calls the hateful person an assassin, then who are these assassins working for?

We find a clue in the only other place where this word *anthrōpoktonos* occurs in the New Testament. Jesus uses it when He is addressing the Jews who said that they believed in God but did not affirm Jesus as Christ:

*You are of your father the devil, and the lusts of your father you will do. He was a **murderer** from the beginning, and abode not in the truth, because there is no truth in him.* (John 8:44)

That word *"murderer"* is the same that is in found in 1 John 3:15! Whoever hates his brother or sister is doing the same murderous work as the father of lies. Unfortunately, the devil has many people in the church unknowingly doing his dirty work for him. These modern-day assassins have traded in their lances and daggers for gossip and slander. They operate with stealth and agility. They hide themselves behind the veil of anonymity and strike their victims down with the movement of their tongue.

If there is one thing that the church needs to reconsider, it is how we show love toward one another. Jesus said, *"By this shall all men know that you are My disciples, if you have love one to another"* (John 13:35). In a previous chapter, I posed the question: do you work for the devil? What if I told you that every time you spoke or entertained slander you were operating in hate? How would that change your outlook?

SATAN'S LIE: KILLING A PERSON'S CHARACTER IS NOT A BIG SIN.

#THEASSASSINSCREED

Character Assassins

You might think that the analogy of the assassin is quite extreme, but I want you to consider what happens when we speak against someone else or someone speaks against us. A *person* may not physically die when they are gossiped about, but *something* definitely dies. Have you considered that somebody's character can be slain even though they themselves may still be alive? People who make it their business to speak evil of others are what I call character assassins. They are spiritual hit men, who go about destroying the reputation of others. I have seen entire blogs and so-called Christian magazines dedicated to assassinating the characters of Christian ministers, worship leaders, and other public figures. Jesus' words apply to them: *"You are of your father the devil…. He was a murderer from the beginning"* (John 8:44).

Make no mistake, those who assassinate characters and reputations are working for the devil. He was a murderer from the very beginning! I always wondered why the devil was kicked out of heaven and punished so severely, but if you consider the implications of his offense, the punishment suited the crime perfectly. He committed the capital crime of murder in his heart. He had the audacity to speak against the character and reputation of God Himself. Can you believe this? If God dealt with Satan in such severe wrath, how shall we escape severe consequences for speaking against our brothers and sisters in Christ, who are made in the image of our heavenly Father?

The character assassin operates according to a creed that usually involves a spirit of duplicity, a spirit of prosecution, and a critical spirit.

The Spirit of Duplicity

Many years ago, I had a very interesting experience. I was speaking with a fellow church member about some things that were bothersome to me, many of which involved him. The conversation was very heated as I expressed my grievances toward him and another brother in the church. After hours, we finally came to a resolution. I apologized for my attitude toward him, and he apologized for his behavior. We finished the conversation on very good terms.

But the next day, I saw him at the church with this other brother who was obviously still very angry with me. Then this other brother referenced something that I had stated in the conversation—that he hadn't even been in! I was so bothered by the fact that the situation had appeared to have been resolved only to be discussed afterward with a third party in such a manner that it spread further offense.

This is what I call the spirit of duplicity. Duplicity is deceitfulness or double-dealing. On the one hand, I was told that everything was resolved, yet on the other hand, the offense was communicated to a third party.

Now, I present this situation not to portray myself as perfect but to convey how duplicity can enter so quickly into a relationship. Many, many people have a double tongue. If you have an argument with Sister Betty, and she comes back and apologizes to you, then you go and tell Sister Jane about the argument, this is absolutely sinful and duplicitous. You accepted Sister Betty's apology and the situation should have been in the past. But when you bring it up with Sister Jane and emphasize the difficulties and problems while omitting the resolution to the situation, then you are engaging in ungodly behavior. I cannot tell you how many times I have witnessed this behavior in the church.

SATAN'S LIE:
EVERY CHURCH NEEDS A SNIPER.
#THEASSASSINSCREED

On the contrary, listen to what the Bible commands that we do:

These are the things that you shall do; speak you every man the truth to his neighbor; execute the judgment of truth and peace in your gates. (Zechariah 8:16)

The Bible goes further in the book of Ephesians and commands us:

Wherefore putting away lying, speak every man truth with his neighbor: for we are members one of another. (Ephesians 4:25)

Double Jeopardy

In legal terms, when someone is prosecuted twice for the same offense, it is referred to as "double jeopardy." Many believers are prosecuting their brothers or sisters twice for the same offense. Anytime you rehearse a painful or hurtful situation to others that has been supposedly resolved, you are committing double jeopardy.

I have been guilty of this. I can remember going to a particular family and apologizing for some things that I had done to them (even though they were also guilty of some offenses against me). I felt led of the Holy Spirit to take the "higher road" and apologize. Afterward, I remember thinking and even rehearsing some things that they did to me in the past. The Lord convicted my heart. He said, "How can you go and apologize and then turn around and think badly of the people you apologized to?"

Don't we all tend to do this? For example, a wife goes to her husband and apologizes for the way she speaks to him, and when she is done apologizing he says, "Thank you!" She then gets angry with him because he didn't apologize too! This creates a spiral-down effect and brings her right back to the initial offense.

You can counteract this tendency by looking at your heart before you apologize. Ask yourself, *Do I really mean what I say? Am I just apologizing to receive an apology? Have I really offended the person who has wounded or hurt me?* If you are going to have healthy, sustainable relationships, you must learn to let go of the past. You must learn to live in the present! Stop rehearsing negative experiences and "prosecuting" others in your heart and mind!

WE MUST OPERATE IN A SPIRIT OF TRUTH IF WE WANT TO UNMASK THE ACCUSER AND WALK IN VICTORY.

Unfortunately, spiritual leaders are guiltier of this than most. In many cases, pastors and leaders speak about their parishioners in an attempt to vent and release the stress of ministry. Though their motives are usually not sinister, this practice can be very destructive. Remember, it is impossible to speak unlovingly and negatively about someone behind their back and still have a healthy relationship with that person. As my wife always says, "We only have one heart!" Many pastors operate in double-mindedness. On the one hand they say they love and treasure the sheep, then on the other hand they complain about how irritated they are by them. A double mind produces a double tongue, which facilitates a double life! The Bible admonishes us to be single-eyed (or single minded) as it will cause us to be *"full of light"* (Matthew 6:22). Conversely, if we are double-minded, our whole body (and life) will be full of darkness. Beloved, God does not want us to walk in darkness. Let us be single-minded and walk in unconditional love.

Spiritual Sleeper Cells

There's a price to pay for double-mindedness. Let me explain. The thought that someone could live a double life has always fascinated me, and so of course I love espionage movies! I grew up on James Bond and films like *The Saint*. The concept of secret agents was always so intriguing to me. Through these spy movies, I became familiar with sleeper cells, essentially a secretive group of spies or terrorist agents that remain inactive within a target population until ordered. Sometimes sleeper cells lead normal lives for years until it is time for them to be activated. Then when they are, *bam!* Suddenly no one is safe.

The same is true of many people in the church who are harboring offense in their hearts. They are spiritual sleeper cells! They sing in the choir. They act on the usher board. They volunteer in children's ministry, but they have a deep, dark, secret in their heart: offense! They have scores of unresolved conflicts built up inside. Unfortunately, most don't even realize their own spiritual condition, and as a result, the Accuser of the brethren can activate them at any time. When the devil wants to cause a church split, he uses sleepers to do it. When he wants moral failure to destroy the reputation of a pastor, he uses sleepers to do it. David said, *"Yea, my own familiar friend, in whom I trusted, which did eat of my bread, has lifted up his heel against me"* (Psalm 41:9).

THE ENEMY USES OUR HURT, PAIN, AND OFFENSE AS A WEAPON TO DIVIDE AND CONQUER!

This is why it is so dangerous to harbor unresolved conflict and offense in your heart. The enemy can and will use it for his own diabolical purposes. It has been some of the people who were closest to me who talked about me the most. The people who insisted that they would never allow anyone to say a negative word about me say the worst things about me.

However, I realize that this is not personal. People just make terrible decisions when they are hurting. I am often reminded of the time my dog was hit by a moving car. I ran to help her, and when I reached to check her wound, she attacked me. I was not aware that when dogs experience severe pain, they revert to their base nature. They are no longer thinking in terms of loyalty, affection, or any other domesticated trait; they are only focusing on their instinct to survive.

This is true of many in the church today! Satan has manipulated them (albeit through pain) to revert to their base, carnal nature. They are activated by rejection, pain, or hurt instead of by love, forgiveness, and longsuffering.

Beloved, God wants to release you from every demonic assignment that would seek to exploit your pain in the name of Jesus. He wants you to be free to love and be loved. He wants the offense in your heart to dissipate so that you are no longer assassins, but nurses; no longer bringing hurt, but relief.

Known by Their Fruit

One of the ways you can easily identify the sleeper cells is by their fruits. (See Matthew 7:20.) You will never find an apple tree with oranges, or a mango tree with watermelons. Why? A tree always produces after its own kind. In the same way, a good tree always produces good fruit. It doesn't matter how innocent a person seems, if their words and actions are contrary to the Word of God, there is a bad seed within.

There was once a beautiful and charismatic woman who came to our church. She was so excited to be at our church, because according to her no church in the state had the presence of God as strong as ours did. One day in a Bible study meeting, she posed the question: why do we need to listen to the pastor, when we can hear from God for ourselves? Though it was posed innocently, the question was saturated with the intention for chaos and confusion. Later, she began to question the order of service, the leadership structure, and even our family dynamics. On the outside she looked the part, but when she bore fruit with her words and actions, they were rotten.

IF YOU ARE NOT OPERATING IN A SPIRIT OF UNITY AND PEACE, THEN YOU ARE OPERATING IN DISUNITY AND CHAOS: GOD IS NOT THE AUTHOR OF CONFUSION!

People like this are called *"evil workers"* in the Bible. Paul the apostle admonishes us in the book of Philippians: *"Beware of evil workers"* (Philippians 3:2). They are the bad-natured, troublesome, injurious, pernicious, and destructive. They go from church to church talking about their negative experiences in previous churches. Yet they never disclose whether *they* were the source of these negative encounters. Often, they are seeking some sort of validation or affirmation that condones their inability to stay in one church.

The Bible tells us, that all things are to be done in decency and in order: *"For God is not the author of confusion, but of peace, as in all churches* of the saints" (1 Corinthians 14:33). The word "confusion" here is a very interesting word. It comes from the Greek word *akatastasia*, which means *instability*. One of the signs that someone is a potential "evil worker" is spiritual and emotional instability. You will find that the people who are the most negative and critical are often the most unstable. They gravitate toward and engage in slander and gossip because there is a deep vacuum within their own spiritual and emotional life and they attempt to fill this void with negativity. They often accuse others in order to excuse themselves of the deep guilt, shame, and condemnation that they feel inside. The sure cure for gossip and slander is a sense of purpose and fulfillment. You cannot be filled with purpose and negativity simultaneously. If you walk in the Spirit, you will not fulfill the lust of the flesh!

The Critical Spirit

Many years ago, I was holding a service in a hotel meeting room when I noticed a visitor walk in the door. After the service, he introduced himself to me as a minister. He expressed his appreciation for the message and the service overall. The next service he was sitting in the front row. The more I spoke with him, the more I noticed that he was someone with ministry experience. Then I noticed that he would pull people to the side and "prophesy" to them. I didn't say anything about it but it made me very uncomfortable.

He then began to advise me that I needed to incorporate a discipleship method in the church that only he understood. He told me that I didn't know anything about discipleship but he had tons of experience and expertise in this area. He told me that the services were too long and that with his help the ministry would do really well. The next time I spoke with him after the service, he began to say negative things about several different pastors in our area. One in particular was a personal friend. I said to him, "That's my friend!" He looked at me with shock. I told him that I was not looking for his help and that he should go on to another ministry.

This person had what I call a critical spirit. Maybe you know someone like this. They criticize the décor, the preaching, the length of the service, and anything else that they can identify. You would think their spiritual lives are superior, but this is usually not the case. In fact, in most cases, their lives are far from perfection, or even stability, for that matter.

Criticism often leads to cynicism. The more we speak negatively of others, the more we will adopt a philosophy that others are negative. However, I want us to concentrate on the fact that the Accuser of the brethren is the one motivating the critical spirit. Criticism distracts us from the positive and valuable things all around us. As the elders in my community would often say, "If you don't have anything good to say, don't say anything at all!" Criticism also keeps us in denial of our own frailty. What would have happened if I allowed the aforementioned gentleman to have influence in the church? It would have been a disaster! What was his track record of success? Who had he mentored? Where were his disciples? He had none, because he was too busy criticizing to be successful in any real endeavor. He was a frail believer.

SATAN'S LIE:
YOU COULD PROBABLY DO
A BETTER JOB THAN THE PASTOR.
#THEASSASSINSCREED

It is the offended heart that facilitates the critical spirit. When we give way to the critical spirit, we cannot hear the Holy Spirit. A critical spirit once bound me as well. I would sit in services, just judging the preacher. One such service I will never forget. A female preacher was speaking to a large crowd. She had long fingernails and what looked like a prom dress. She was loud and boisterous—and I did not even believe in female preachers! God sure has a sense of humor. I was sitting there thinking about her service with a critical spirit when this woman spoke to my wife and me the most accurate words of knowledge that I had ever received. Needless to say, I don't have a problem with women being preachers anymore. My critical spirit toward her almost cost me my blessing and my future.

The Law of Sowing and Reaping

We will reap what we sow, especially when it comes to slander and gossip. Listen to what the Bible says in Galatians 6:

Brethren, if a man be overtaken in a fault, you which are spiritual, restore such a one in the spirit of meekness; considering yourself, lest you also be tempted. Bear you one another's burdens, and so fulfill the law of Christ.… Be not deceived; God is not mocked: for whatsoever a man sows, that shall he also reap. For he that sows to his flesh shall of the flesh reap corruption; but he that sows to the Spirit shall of the Spirit reap life everlasting. (Galatians 6:1–2, 7–8)

We often hear people teach that we will reap what we sow, which is definitely a universal truth. However, in the book of Galatians, this principle is taught in a particular context. The apostle Paul is making specific reference to the first two verses of the chapter: *"Brethren, if a man be overtaken in a fault, you which are spiritual, restore such a one in the spirit of meekness; considering yourself, lest you also be tempted."* The law of sowing and reaping applies to every area of our lives, but is especially true in relationships. What you criticize others for, you will be judged by in exponential measure. The church has a spiritual obligation to restore those who have been overtaken in a fault, not to assassinate their character.

WHAT YOU CRITICIZE OTHERS FOR, YOU WILL BE JUDGED BY IN EXPONENTIAL MEASURE.

You may say, "Well, that's the price they have to pay for failing!" I have a question: what price do you pay for your failures? God does not need your help judging, gossiping, and criticizing, but He could use your help restoring. The problem with slander and gossip is that it makes no room or allowance for restoration to take place. One of the things about our church that I am very proud of is the culture of restoration. We believe it is our duty to facilitate healing and restoration to those who have fallen or been wounded by the church. In fact, we are one of the few churches in our city where it is common for people to leave the church (sometimes on bad terms) and come back; and when they return, they are welcomed with open arms. One of the reasons why I make it a habit to extend compassion to others is that I am fully aware that I have needed and will need the same compassion.

In one particular case, a family in our church left out of offense. They accused us of preaching against them. I had no idea that they felt this way as I never even considered them in my messages. However, they decided to leave. Several months later, they came back to the church. After visiting for several weeks, they left again, citing spiritual abuse as a possible culprit. Interestingly, they came back a third time and, in a dramatic act of humility, bowed before my wife and I and asked for forgiveness with tears in their eyes. This restoration touched us deeply and left an indelible imprint on our hearts.

The thing to note is that by God's grace we never spoke a negative word about this family. We never discussed what happened with anyone in the church and we never attempted to assassinate his or her character. As a result, they were able to return and see the relationship restored. What would have happened if we went around telling everybody that they offended us? If would have been difficult, if not impossible, to restore fellowship with this precious family. One of the lessons that I have learned in ministry is that every soul is precious to God. Every person is valuable and significant in His eyes. This is why He takes it very personally when we speak against one of His children.

The nature of the Accuser is always condemnation, but the nature of the Creator is always restoration. If you have participated in slander, gossip, or character assassination, repent immediately and ask God to purify your heart and give you His perspective on life and the church.

For Discussion

1. How do we assassinate the characters of others? How can we be nurses instead?

2. Should we only repent and apologize if we know the other person will apologize, too? Why or why not?

3. Has your church or family ever fallen prey to the critical spirit? How did you fight it? Consider Luke 6:37 and James 2:1–4.

Testimony

I used to be very critical of others! Nothing and no one was ever really good enough for me. I regularly spoke about others and their sins and imperfections. This behavior was completely justified in my mind—until God began to show me areas of bitterness in my own life. The truth was that the impatience I displayed toward others was really a veiled impatience and intolerance for my own sins and imperfections. My difficulty in loving others was nothing more than a manifestation of my own inability to receive God's love for me. After years of being judgmental and critical, I finally forgave myself and was able to experience the unconditional love of God. Once I received His love for me, I could freely extend love to others. —*Pastor T.*

Prayer

Father, in the name of Jesus, I thank You for Your mercy and I appreciate Your lovingkindness. Your Word declares that whoever hates his brother is a murderer and does not have eternal life abiding in him. I recognize the severity of Your Word in this area, and I ask You to forgive me for operating in hatred in any area of my life. Thank You, Lord, for teaching me how to walk in love toward everyone. I repent for participating in the assassination of any person's character, and I forgive anyone who has attempted to assassinate my character. I declare that I walk in the Spirit of truth and that through Your Word, I unmask the Accuser of the brethren. I declare that I walk in victory in every area of my life, especially my thoughts and my words. In the name of Jesus, I pray.

Amen!

10

SATAN'S AGENDA

Lest Satan should get an advantage of us: for we are not ignorant of his devices. (2 Corinthians 2:11)

Throughout this book, we have made the agenda of the enemy abundantly clear: he desires to steal, kill, and destroy. I believe that God has given me the assignment of exposing the wicked one for who he truly is: a liar and a deceiver. In 2 Corinthians 2:11, Paul exclaims that Satan will not take advantage of those in the church because they are not ignorant of his evil purposes. This verse carries an assurance; if we know his devices, Satan shall not gain an advantage over us. However, this verse also contains a warning; we cannot be ignorant of his devices, or Satan will take advantage of us!

Many inside the church are ignorant and Satan is using them even right this minute. How can I make such a claim? Because I see thousands of churchgoers all over the globe attacking one another rather than recognizing and exposing the devices of the devil. They exhaust their energy fighting, gossiping, and slandering the body of Christ. They do not recognize that they are advancing the kingdom of darkness. Most people don't even realize they are working for Satan! Sometimes he recruits well-meaning Christians to carry out his agenda to steal, kill, and destroy. Beware that you are not assisting the enemy's plans. Open your spiritual eyes and check to make sure the enemy is not using you or anyone in your life. God opened my eyes to Satan's agenda in a dramatic vision of snakes.

Snakes in the Church

Several years ago, I had a vivid dream. I was in the middle of a church service. People were streaming through the doors into the building. The sanctuary was filled with praise and excitement. As people continued to enter the sanctuary in my dream, I realized that something was wrong. Something told me to go outside and check the perimeter. As I walked outside, I noticed that there were snakes on the sidewalk. They were chatting with the people outside. It dawned on me that these snakes were discouraging people from entering the building. I began to stamp on the snakes all over the sidewalk to kill them, but then I looked up and saw that there weren't just snakes on the sidewalk, the grass was crawling with them, too!

A thought came to me in my dream: how many more snakes are *inside* the church? When I woke up from this dream, I received a startling revelation. There are many people in the church who are unknowingly advancing the kingdom of darkness. Pastors and leaders must be careful not to tolerate them!

I refer to these individuals as snakes in the church not to demean any particular person but to accentuate the severity of this issue. In the Bible, serpents are used to illustrate cunning, deception, and manipulation. They are capable of poisoning their victims with a venomous snakebite. The same is true of snakes in the church; they speak out the poisonous venom of slander and gossip. They infect their victims with negative words. Offense is poisonous. It is contagious; even when you don't know you have it, it can infect you.

A House Divided Cannot Stand

Snakes are also capable of camouflage. They slither through the grass unseen by the naked eye. So it is with snakes inside the church: they blend in with the environment and are almost impossible to tell apart from the worshippers. Eventually, however, their true nature is revealed.

One day God showed me that there were people in the church who were deterring other from connecting to our ministry. After a time of fasting and prayer, the truth was exposed. Several people came to me and said that they loved the church and they loved the worship, but they could no longer tolerate the offensive behavior of certain individuals. I discovered that these were, by their words and persuasion, disconnecting people from the church.

SATAN'S LIE:
UNITY IS IMPOSSIBLE, SO WHY TRY?
#SATANSAGENDA

This was a very frustrating ordeal! Here I was preaching my heart out, and there were snakes destroying the work that was being done. There is nothing worse than building something and discovering that it is being dismantled right under your nose. God is not pleased with this kind of behavior. We prayerfully dealt with the strife in the church and the individuals causing it.

I have said before and will say again: God is a God of unity! Division never leads to victory! Jesus told us as much:

> But when the Pharisees heard it, they said, This fellow does not cast out devils, but by Beelzebub the prince of the devils. And Jesus knew their thoughts, and said to them, Every kingdom divided against itself is brought to desolation; and every city or house divided against itself shall not stand: and if Satan cast out Satan, he is divided against himself; how shall then his kingdom stand? And if I by Beelzebub cast out devils, by whom do your children cast them out? therefore they shall be your judges. (Matthew 12:24–27)

Can you imagine the kingdom of darkness being more united than the church? God forbid! Yet countless people are absolutely oblivious to the fact that Satan is perpetuating strife and division to render the church ineffective. It is sad to think that the most segregated time of the week is Sunday morning. The truth is that we must fight for unity. No matter how hurt, wounded, or offended you are, it is never worth the cost of division. Beloved, division is chaos! The Bible says that a house divided cannot stand. How can we stand against the perversion and darkness pervading our culture if we are not united? The answer is, *we can't!* Let us come together and resist the devil!

Spiritual Leaven

One of my favorite delicacies is a yeast roll. They are simply delicious! Especially with a hint of butter and honey, although now that I am older, I can't afford to eat as many as I would like. There is a spiritual principle hidden in this delectable treat. In his epistle to the Galatians, Paul the apostle admonishes the church saying: *"This persuasion comes not of Him that calls you. A little leaven leavens the whole lump"* (Galatians 5:8–9). He wrote this to address the Judaizers (legalistic Christians subverting the faith of the Gentile converts) in the church who were causing division. He said that their persuasion did not come from God. Beloved, God has no tolerance for strife and division. If you are associating yourself with someone who engages in this behavior, you need to cease and desist immediately. Pastors, if you discover that someone on your staff or leadership team is causing strife, you need to speak with them immediately. Why? The Bible says a little leaven leavens the whole lump. Simply put, sin is like the yeast in a batch of dough for rolls: just one little teaspoon can spread rapidly through the large batch and change the make-up of the whole dough.

OPENING YOUR HEART TO OFFENSE WILL ULTIMATELY POISON YOUR SOUL, AND RENDER YOU INEFFECTIVE IN THE KINGDOM OF GOD.

The Bible goes further to say we should purge out the old leaven, in order that we may be a new lump. (See 1 Corinthians 5:6.) This is especially true when it comes to slander and gossip. The longer you tolerate it, the faster it spreads. Yet the church has seemed to tolerate this sinister device of the devil for far too long. The Bible commands us to purge out the old leaven.

Poisonous Pity Parties

A sneakier and more passive form of fomenting strife is to throw pity parties. Beware of people who enlarge your pain rather than encouraging you to be healed and move on. These prognosticators are always willing and ready to talk about all the negative things that may be happening in your life, but they rarely bring healthy solutions.

SATAN'S LIE:
YOU CAN THROW A
PITY PARTY IF YOU WANT TO!
#SATANSAGENDA

There was a time when I wore my heart on my sleeve. I hate to admit it, but it is true. I would be debilitated by rejection. In one particular instance, I was coming out of a church service and someone whom I really liked refused to speak to me. It seemed as if they were giving me the silent treatment. I was so hurt by this! On the way home, my neighbor, who had kindly given me a ride, saw my distress and asked what was wrong. I told them that this particular person did not speak to me after church. My neighbor, instead of helping me to climb out my pit of despair and giving me a helpful dose of reality, threw a party inside the pit. He began to participate in the pain that I was feeling by telling me how wrong the person was and how inconsiderate their actions were. He told me that I was a good person, and that others just didn't know my worth. This all seemed fine on the exterior, but deep within, it left me feeling empty.

This is what I call a poisonous pity party. There are people in our lives who participate in our pain in an effort to make us feel better, but ultimately hurt us more than they help us. These are the people you call when things don't work out the way you think they should. You tell them how the pastor hurt your feelings, and they say he was so wrong for doing that! Little do you know that they are helping to administer the enemy's poison into your heart. This is equivalent to spiritual euthanasia. It is time for you to fire the Dr. Kevorkian's in your life! We must make a conscious decision to not allow ourselves to be contaminated by the enemy's poison.

Don't get me wrong; we all need a person in our lives we can talk to when things are difficult or challenging, but we must make sure that the voices that speak into our lives will always point us back to the truth of God's Word, not make matters worse.

Marriages are especially prone to poisonous pity parties. When you exacerbate the hurts and wounds of your spouse, it makes your spouse actually less able to deal with the real problem. I have witnessed couples leave churches prematurely because they, as a couple, made each other feel worse and worse about the situation instead of seeking outside help.

I call this Job's wife syndrome. When Job was in his darkest hour, his wife should have been a voice of peace, hope, and consolation for her husband. Instead, she was a voice of insanity. She told Job to curse God and die. Now that's some pillow-talk for you!

When couples rehearse their pain with each other, they simply make themselves even more bitter and resentful. By voicing accusation after accusation in the privacy of their home, they are digging themselves into a pit of pain and despair. This is why it is so important to surround yourself with people who will hold you accountable to the truth and not just agree with your every grievance. You need people who will help you to stay balanced and honest with yourself. The last thing you need when you are hurting is a yes man.

A true friend will help you answer questions about difficult situations, such as: Who was behind this? Was it a systematic problem or was it simply the actions of one uncompassionate church member? Was the pastor negligent? If our needs aren't being met, have we told anyone about it? As husbands and wives we must make sure that we are ministering hope and healing to our spouses, not encouraging them to take the road of bitterness and offense.

Keep Your Love On!

Motel 6's popular ad on the radio and on the television ended with the tagline, "We'll leave the light on for ya." This suggests a welcoming and friendly atmosphere. What would happen if we adopted this same mentality when it comes to Christian relationships? What if we determine to always keep the light on?

The Bible says that he that loves his brother walks in the light. However, he that hates his brother walks around in darkness and cannot see where he stumbles. (See 1 John 2:9–11.) Could it be possible that much of the confusion and the chaos that we are seeing in the church is the direct result of a lack of love?

I remember hearing an interesting story. There were two families in a church. On the outside, both of these families were very similar. They both attended church regularly. They both were very involved in ministry. Both families were sincere in their desire to please God. However, one family seemed to be more blessed than the other. The other family noticed that this family was always being blessed and prospering in everything that they did. One day, the father of the family who was not as blessed went to God in prayer. He asked God why they were not prospering as much as this other family. Expecting a profound theological answer, he was shocked by the simplicity of what he heard. The answer was *love!* God told him that the difference in these two families was their love walk.

In the famous passage on love, 1 Corinthians 13, we learn that love is both powerful and necessary. Why is this so important to our discussion about offense? Because, simply put, a loving believer will not give rise to offense!

> *Though I speak with the tongues of men and of angels, and have not charity, I am become as sounding brass, or a tinkling cymbal. And though I have the gift of prophecy, and understand all mysteries, and all knowledge; and though I have all faith, so that I could remove mountains, and have not charity, I am nothing. And though I bestow all my goods to feed the poor, and though I give my body to be burned, and have not charity, it profits me nothing. Charity suffers long, and is kind; charity envies not; charity vaunts not itself, is not puffed up, does not behave itself unseemly, seeks not her own, is not easily provoked, thinks no evil; rejoices not in iniquity, but rejoices in the truth; bears all things, believes all things, hopes all things, endures all things.* (1 Corinthians 13:1–7)

It is very important to note that the Corinthian church was one of the most gifted in the New Testament. They understood how to prophesy and speak in tongues. They operated in the power of the Holy Spirit. Yet the apostle Paul saw fit to teach them about the importance of love. Why? The simple truth is that without love, nothing else really works. In fact, without love, nothing else really matters!

What is love? The word used for *love* here is *agape*, which is loosely interpreted as divine love. There are several types of love mentioned in the Bible. There is *phileo*, which is brotherly love. There is *eros*, which is intimate or erotic love, and then there is *agape*. *Agape* is the same quality of love that God possesses within Himself and displays toward mankind. This is the love of John 3:16: *"For God so **loved** the world, that He gave His only begotten Son, that whosoever believes in Him should not perish, but have everlasting life."* In other words, the love of God is selfless and sacrificial. He commended His love toward us in that while we were yet sinners, Christ died.

Can you imagine the extent of God's lovingkindness toward us? He *died* for us when we were in our worse state—yet we often demand perfection from others before we will give them the time of day. Once we get a revelation of the unconditional love of God toward all of us, we will be able to walk in grace and compassion toward one another. Satan's agenda is to steal, kill, and destroy, but the Lamb's agenda is that we would have life and have it in abundance. (See John 10:10.)

For Discussion

1. What is Satan's agenda for every believer? What do you think his agenda is for you in particular?

2. What's the difference between "weeping with those who weep" (see Romans 12:15) and throwing a poisonous pity party?

3. What are some ways you can "keep the light on" in your life? What tends to turn the light off?

Practicum

1. Consider the people who have apologized to you and expressed their sorrow over what has happened. Did you let the offense go or is

it still festering in your heart? If it's still there, release it with the freedom that comes from being a child of God!

2. "Criticism leads to cynicism." What are you cynical about? Family, church, friends, your job, the government? Does it come from a spirit of criticism? Pray over how you can build up, not tear down.

3. Gather a group of believers and pray a prayer of unity over the church of Jesus Christ. Pray for unity despite personal, doctrinal, geographical, racial, cultural, political, and all other differences. Declare Galatians 3:28 over the gathering.

Testimony

The devil attacked my marriage in a very serious way. There was unfaithfulness and hurt in my relationship with my spouse. I felt betrayed and rejected. The enemy told me to walk away from my marriage. He told me that my spouse did not love me and that it was futile to try and preserve my union.

While praying one day, the Lord said, "Stand on my Word and fight for your marriage!" Even though the Accuser was bombarding me, I made a faith decision that day to stand on the Word of God. I began to confess God's promises over my union. I allowed the Word of God to drown out the voice of the Accuser. Through God's grace, I forgave my spouse completely and our marriage began to heal.

Now I have a peace and a joy that I can't begin to describe. Ironically, my spouse and I are closer and more in love than we have ever been before.   —Mrs. Gina

Prayer

Father, in the name of Jesus, I thank You for the power of Your unfailing love and the revelation of Your Word. I know that You desire for me to walk in my purpose; therefore, I connect my faith to the truth of Your Word. I ask that You expose every snake

operating in my life or in my church, and that You bring deliverance immediately. Your Word declares that a house divided cannot stand; therefore, I choose not to be an agent of division. Instead, I choose to be an agent of unity. I close my heart to any and all offenses so that my soul will not be poisoned. Teach me how to keep my love on every single day. In the name of Jesus.

Amen!

11

THE GRACE SPACE

Let us therefore come boldly to the throne of grace, that we may obtain mercy, and find grace to help in time of need. (Hebrews 4:16)

When was the last time you went to the emergency room and the staff said that you were too sick to be admitted? The hospital is *exactly* where you're supposed to go when you're sick. Right? But imagine a bunch of patients wheeling themselves out of the hospital, untreated, perhaps even worse off than they were before, all because the doctors asked a few questions, took a few tests, watched a few behaviors, and then decided, "Well, you're just too far gone. We can't help you!"

And in the same way, the church is *exactly* where you're supposed to go when you're hurting. But too many people leave churches because they don't receive any help there! This is the direct result of a lack of grace.

Grace and Peace

Many years ago, the Lord gave me the name of our church. He told me it must be "Grace & Peace Global Fellowship" because it would be a place where grace reigned. He told me that all churches should similarly have an atmosphere of grace. What did this mean to me? All the world! You see, I was raised in a very legalistic environment. I was well-acquainted with correction, but knew very little about compassion. It was not until several years ago that I received a true biblical revelation of grace.

As I began to explore this concept of grace more deeply, I realized that there has been a serious deficiency of grace in the church, not theologically, but relationally. The Bible says, *"And the Word was made flesh, and dwelt among us, (and we beheld His glory, the glory as of the only begotten of the Father,) full of grace and truth"* (John 1:14). Jesus was full of grace and truth, and this quality of grace and truth characterized His earthly ministry. He went to the sick, the lame, the broken, the immoral, and the lost—the people who are often neglected in our modern ministries. This was a very revolutionary concept for me. This does not mean that we condone or accept sin, but it does mean that we accept sinners. It is very easy to focus on the faults of others, but it is often more challenging to love people to life. The Lord told me that once people had a revelation of grace, they would live in His peace. Hence the name, "Grace & Peace."

The truth is that God cares about relationships. He so desired our fellowship that He sent His Son to redeem the world from sin, the sin that alienated us from intimate fellowship with God.

IF THE ENTIRE REDEMPTIVE PLAN OF GOD HINGED UPON THE RESTORATION OF RELATIONSHIPS, THEN THIS SHOULD BE THE CHURCH'S PRIORITY.

The Bible tells us: *"Put on therefore, as the elect of God, holy and beloved, bowels of mercies, kindness, humbleness of mind, meekness, long-suffering; forbearing one another, and forgiving one another, if any man have a quarrel against any: even as Christ forgave you, so also do you"* (Colossians 3:12–13). What does it mean to *forbear*? The word *forbear* comes from the Greek word *anechō*, which means: to hold up, to sustain, or to endure.

What does forbearance look like? It means to endure or to tolerate. It means there's a grace. I have said it before and I will say it again: the church is far too prone to offense. Why? Because we have tolerated a culture of offense in our modern churches. This is completely antithetical to the biblical culture of forbearance.

Once in college a guy came back to the dorm completely inebriated. He was so drunk he could barely stand, and he looked awful. My friend and I picked him up, put him in our car, and drove him to the hospital. As soon as we arrived they rushed him into ICU. As we were in the waiting room, the doctor came and asked us if we were related to him, and we replied that we were just dorm-mates. She said that our friend had sustained alcohol poisoning, and that if we had come any later, he would be dead. Essentially, when we carried him into the hospital, we sustained him until he was able to get the help he needed. That is what forbearance looks like.

The church must be a place where we forbear, where we make allowance for people to learn and grow, where we sustain people until they get the help that they need. The church must not be a place where we demand perfection. The same is true when it comes to parishioners and their relationships with their pastors. Some people are so easily offended by their leaders that it is a downright shame. They never exercise forbearance toward the spiritual leadership. The moment somebody says or does something that they do not agree with, they are immediately ready to leave. This is not the Spirit of God! Why not? Because God does not treat us this way!

Isn't it ironic that we often demand perfection of others while allowing imperfection in ourselves? We often judge other people based upon their actions and judge ourselves based upon our intentions. In an earlier chapter, we discussed the need for what I call a buffer, or a five-second rule. This means that there must be an internal space in which we make allowances for people's failures and offenses toward us. In other words, don't allow yourself to immediately become offended. When Sister Barbara doesn't speak to you after Sunday school, don't immediately assume that she doesn't like you. If we would endeavor to distinguish, we would find that things are not always what they seem to be.

I can remember a particular situation in which a wonderful woman in the church came to me stating that I should "tell her the truth!" We had had a conversation earlier in the day—right after I'd eaten lunch, I must add. I asked her what she meant by this comment. With tears in her eyes she said, "Tell me the truth; if you want me to leave the church, just say it!" I was beyond puzzled by her words; she was an amazing member of our church! "What do you mean by that?" I exclaimed. She said, "I saw the way that you looked at me when we were talking. You don't like me!" I couldn't hold back a grin as I apologized for my earlier demeanor. I told her that the truth was that I had gas! She then burst into laughter.

The moral of this story is that we should not always assume that someone has a negative sentiment toward us. I call this the grace space. The church should be a space of grace, an area where people are allowed to make mistakes and to show their frailties without criticism, judgment, or condemnation. This does not mean that you won't be corrected. But when you are corrected or rebuked, it should always be done in love.

Debt-Collecting and Grace

Jesus told a parable of a man who owed his lord a huge sum of money. Huge! Even if this man had saved all his salary for a year, he would not be able pay it back. He went to his lord and begged him for mercy. In his compassion, the lord forgave the man his debt in total and released him from all financial obligations. This same man then went and found a fellow servant who owed him a small amount of money. He demanded that this guy pay up, and when the servant couldn't and begged for mercy, he threw him in prison! The lord heard about this and was incensed. He called for the first servant again and rebuked him saying, "I forgave you all your debt and yet you couldn't forgive your fellow servant his debt? I shall cast you into prison until you repay all that was owed." (See Matthew 18:23–35.)

This parable is a perfect picture of the spiritual condition of many people in the body of Christ. They have become spiritual debt collectors. They spend their entire lives collecting debts from others. Not in a financial sense, but in the spiritual and emotional sense. In other words, everyone owes them something. The pastor owes them an explanation for every step he takes. The pastor's spouse owes them for the hasty word spoken six months ago. The ushers owe them for walking down the wrong aisle. The pianist owes them for the musical selection. The couple who started attending another church owes them for leaving. The single mom owes them for missing church sometimes. The elder owes them for not being gracious.

All the while, these debt-collectors don't think they're accountable to anybody! They forget they owe a huge debt to God. The worst part about all of this is that they often spiritualize this dysfunctional mind-set. They do not realize that they are in a prison of guilt, pain, and hurt. It is almost like a woman coming out of an abusive relationship. She subconsciously believes that every other man that she meets will abuse her in the same fashion. As a result, any man she dates has to prove time and time again that he will not hurt her. This can be very emotionally draining for the other party. At some point she must let go of her pain if she wants to enjoy a healthy and fruitful relationship. In the same way, spiritual debt collectors must make the decision that their pain will not dictate the future.

SATAN'S LIE: ONLY SHOW GRACE TO THOSE WHO DESERVE IT.

#THEGRACESPACE

Earlier I mentioned that grace is not just about us rectifying our relationship with God, but it is also about us rectifying our relationships with each other. God did not just come through Jesus to redeem our vertical relationship, He also came to redeem our horizontal relationships. This is why the church is such a vital environment. The Bible tells us to forsake not the assembling of ourselves together. (See Hebrews 10:25.) Why? Because there is something about community that forces us to confront the wounds in our heart. This is absolutely necessary if we want to experience sure restoration in our lives. We will talk a little bit about how to heal from the wounds of the past, but for now I want to explore this notion of grace.

What is grace? Grace is favor and kindness that you did not earn or deserve. The Bible says that God demonstrates His love toward us in that while we were yet sinners Christ died for us. (See Romans 5:8.) In other words, He extended us favor, not based upon our works, but according to His lovingkindness: *"By grace are you saved through faith; and that not of yourselves: it is the gift of God"* (Ephesians 2:8). Everything about our salvific experience is based upon God's gift of grace to us, which we receive by faith.

What if I told you that the same was true of our natural relationships? We must show grace first! The same grace that is necessary to enjoy a favorable relationship with God is necessary to enjoy a healthy relationship with other people, especially within the church.

Yet we find that the opposite is often true. Did you know that the average person only stays in a church for two years or less? Why is this the case? Is it because they move or relocate? Is it because God speaks to them and tells them that their assignment is up? Or is it something else? In most cases, at least in my experience, people leave prematurely as a direct result of offense. They cannot show the grace to others that they receive daily from God. Maybe the pastor preaches something that they find offensive. Maybe one of their fellow church members does something that they deem hurtful. Regardless of how you look at it, offense is usually at the root of every premature disconnection from community.

The Religious Spirit

If you study the gospel accounts, you will find that Jesus was very tough on the Pharisees and the Sadducees. Why? Jesus knew that the religious leaders set the spiritual tone for the people of Israel at that time. Whatever behavior they modeled, the people would follow. Unfortunately, many of their examples went directly against Scripture.

Jesus asked the Pharisees, "*Why behold you the mote that is in your brother's eye, but consider not the beam that is in your own eye?*" (Matthew 7:3). Jesus was asking them, "Why is it that you can so easily see the faults of others and not see your own?" This is the primary characteristic of the religious spirit. People with a religious spirit are often extremely judgmental and hypocritical. They often talk about what others do wrong while not acknowledging their own wrongdoing.

Do you remember the story that Jesus narrated about the two men who went to pray? One of them was a Pharisee and the other a tax collector. The Pharisee told God how righteous he was and how many times he tithed and fasted every week. He focused on his own goodness and righteousness. On the other hand, the tax collector bowed his head to the floor and told God that he was nothing but a sinner and that he was in need of God's mercy. Jesus said that the *hated tax collector* went home justified! (See Luke 18:9–14.) Jesus used this story to illustrate the importance of humility and the danger of self-righteousness.

I do not believe that humility is a matter of always telling God how sinful we are. It's not an exercise in putting ourselves down. Rather, it's an attitude of life wherein we are constantly acknowledging our need for Him. We must live in a perpetual state of appreciation for what God has done for us.

But I am sorry to say that there are many religious Pharisees in our churches. Instead of humility they opt for self-righteousness, and self-righteousness is rooted in pride.

PRIDE IS A VAIN CONCENTRATION ON SELF INSTEAD OF GOD. PRIDE IS THE ROOT OF ALL HYPOCRISY AND SELF-RIGHTEOUSNESS.

The greatest indicator of one's depth of revelation in the area of grace is one's willingness and liberality in extending grace to others. When He was rebuked for showing kindness to a prostitute who was worshipping Him, Jesus responded, *"Her sins, which are many, are forgiven; for she loved much: but to whom little is forgiven, the same loves little"* (Luke 7:47). In other words, Jesus said whoever has been forgiven much loves much. We are gracious in proportion to the grace we have received. If we think that we are righteous like the Pharisee in the parable, we will not see our own need for grace, and we will not extend grace to others.

The Lust for Crucifixion

There is an interesting phenomenon in our culture today. And social media is just making it worse. People enjoy seeing others fail. You might disagree with my statement, but the proof is in the pudding, as they say. The trending topics are usually the most scandalous. I posted a video on Facebook called "My Wife Is in Love with Someone Else." The video ended up going viral and reaching over thirty million people! I was referring to my wife being in love with Jesus, and how that love has helped to strengthen and heal our marriage. But would you believe it, people were offended when they found out that the video had a positive message! They watched it for the scandal and felt cheated when there was no scandal. These are the times in which we live.

However, this is not a new phenomenon. The same people who cried "Hosanna" to Christ were the ones who later screamed "Crucify Him!"

This is the nature of the religious spirit. *To crucify* means to put some-one to death by binding the person to a cross. I don't want to diminish the severity of the fact that hundreds of Christians have *physically* been tortured all over the world, but I want to accentuate a very serious anal-ogy: instead of taking up our cross, we are *spiritually* nailing others to it! Church members are crucifying their pastors, leaders are crucifying their parishioners, husbands are crucifying their wives—and vice versa on each one of those too! We pray that we would be able to raise the dead, while killing the living by assassinating their character and reputation.

Isn't it funny how a person can tell you how much they love their church and their pastor, and the following week exclaim how horrible the church is—just because they've been offended? There is a part of hu-man nature that wants vindication. We want to see people suffer for the wrong they do to us. But Jesus modeled a totally different paradigm.

JESUS CAME TO GIVE LIFE NOT DEATH, TO HEAL NOT TO SICKEN, TO JUSTIFY AND NOT CONDEMN.

There is a very powerful story in the Bible that illustrates the grace shown by our Lord:

> *And it came to pass, when the time was come that He should be received up, He steadfastly set His face to go to Jerusalem, and sent messengers before His face: and they went, and entered into a village of the Samaritans, to make ready for Him. And they did not receive Him, because His face was as though He would go to Jerusalem. And when His disciples James and John saw this, they said, Lord, will You that we command fire to come down from heaven, and con-sume them, even as Elijah did? But He turned, and rebuked them, and said, You know not what manner of spirit you are of. For the Son of man is not come to destroy men's lives, but to save them. And they went to another village.* (Luke 9:51–56)

The disciples were seeking vindication for the disrespect and the spite shown toward Jesus, and they asked if fire could come down and consume their enemies. Jesus rebuked them! He said that they were of a wrong spirit. He said that He did not come to destroy lives but to save them. This must be at the heart of everything we do. Mercy triumphs against judgment, every time.

The Prodigal Son

You are probably very familiar with the biblical account of the prodigal son. We have heard this story many times in Sunday school:

> *And He said, A certain man had two sons: and the younger of them said to his father, Father, give me the portion of goods that falls to me. And he divided to them his living. And not many days after the younger son gathered all together, and took his journey into a far country, and there wasted his substance with riotous living.*
>
> *And when he had spent all, there arose a mighty famine in that land; and he began to be in want. And he went and joined himself to a citizen of that country; and he sent him into his fields to feed swine. And he would fain have filled his belly with the husks that the swine did eat: and no man gave to him. And when he came to himself, he said, How many hired servants of my father's have bread enough and to spare, and I perish with hunger! I will arise and go to my father, and will say to him, Father, I have sinned against heaven, and before you, and am no more worthy to be called your son: make me as one of your hired servants. And he arose, and came to his father.*
>
> *But when he was yet a great way off, his father saw him, and had compassion, and ran, and fell on his neck, and kissed him. And the son said to him, Father, I have sinned against heaven, and in your sight, and am no more worthy to be called your son.*
>
> *But the father said to his servants, Bring forth the best robe, and put it on him; and put a ring on his hand, and shoes on his feet: and bring here the fatted calf, and kill it; and let us eat, and be merry: For this my son was dead, and is alive again; he was lost, and is found. And they began to be merry.* (Luke 15:11–24)

I want to highlight a specific aspect of the account. We know that Jesus used the term *"a certain man,"* which suggests that this was not a parable, but an actual occurrence. We also know that the punishment in that culture for dishonoring your biological father was death. (See Proverbs 20:20.) To ask for your inheritance in that culture was like saying, "Move over, dad. I wish you were dead." The prodigal son committed this monstrosity of asking for his inheritance early, then spent all of his money on riotous living. He began to regret his decision. He looked from where he was, a pigpen, up to his father's house (a house on the hill signifies wealth, so his dad was probably wealthy). He knew that his father was a gracious master, and that even the servants in his father's house had more to eat than he did. He decided to ask to be a humble servant to his father—since he knows he deserves nothing more.

But as the son makes his way to the father's house, his father sees him from a distance and *runs* to him. Now, this was not normal! Men of prominence in the East never ran anywhere because running would expose their legs and compromise their dignity. Yet, out of his great love for his son, the father ran to him, covered him, and embraced him. Even though the law demanded justice, the mercy and love of the father offered forgiveness instead.

Think about two details: First, the father asked that a robe be put around his son and a ring placed on his finger. This signified restoration. The son was accepted back into the family and given a signet or seal that indicated his covenant with the father. Second thing: before there could be restoration, there had to be repentance. The son had to confront his father and repent. This is why it is so important for us to humble ourselves before God and others and communicate where we have wronged or been wronged. The son had a change of mind that produced a change in his attitude and actions. And his father was willing and waiting to restore his son to dignity and decency.

THERE MUST BE REPENTANCE BEFORE THERE CAN BE RESTORATION.

Even though you may have read or heard this story before, I wanted to remind you that our heavenly Father is in the business of restoration, too. He doesn't expose our sin, but covers it, welcomes us back into the family with open arms, and protects us from public scorn and condemnation. Would you do the same for your son? Why then would we do any less for people within the body of Christ? Whenever we reduce someone to their failure, we take away their decency and their dignity. At times we even rob them of their humanity.

Grace says, what you have done will not dictate your future. Grace facilitates true repentance. Grace makes room for the lost to come home, and the fallen to be restored.

Lessons from the Elder Brother

There is yet another aspect to this story that we don't often consider: the elder brother. Why is the elder brother such a significant part of our conversation? Because the elder brother represents the religious community, the church.

> Now his elder son was in the field: and as he came and drew near to the house, he heard music and dancing.
>
> And he called one of the servants, and asked what these things meant. And he said to him, Your brother is come; and your father has killed the fatted calf, because he has received him safe and sound.
>
> And he was angry, and would not go in: therefore came his father out, and entreated him. And he answering said to his father, Lo, these many years do I serve you, neither transgressed I at any time your commandment: and yet you never gave me a kid, that I might make merry with my friends: But as soon as this your son was come, which has devoured your living with harlots, you have killed for him the fatted calf. And he said to him, Son, you are ever with me, and all that I have is yours.
>
> It was meet that we should make merry, and be glad: for this your brother was dead, and is alive again; and was lost, and is found.
>
> (Luke 15:25–32)

It is clear from the text that the elder brother was disturbed. Once he discovered that his younger brother was not only accepted back into the family, but was being *celebrated*, he immediately demanded an answer. He was angry! He was thinking, *All these years I've served my father and he has never made a big deal about me, but when my brother scorns him and runs away and comes back, suddenly he gets a big party?* He began to articulate his track record of righteousness. He reminded the father that in all the years he had been with him, he had never sinned or transgressed against his father. It is abundantly clear that the elder brother wanted justice. He desired to be vindicated! Yet, he clearly misunderstood the spiritual ramifications of what was taking place. His father explained to him, "*Your brother was dead, and is alive again.*"

I want you to think about the magnitude of that statement. We know that the younger brother was not dead physically, but he *was* dead spiritually. In other words, the brother was dead the moment his heart rebelled against his father's house.

Many times we are not aware of the spiritual condition of those around us. We fail to rejoice in their periods of blessing because we do not know where they're coming out of. If someone told you that your relative died, I am pretty sure you wouldn't say, "Well, serves him right." Why? Because they are your relative. You have a relationship with them. They are significant to you! You want them to be blessed and healthy. Similarly, in the church today, we ought not to be chagrined when blessing and favor come upon those whom, in our eyes, are totally undeserving! If you feel that temptation, ask yourself, *Do I think I am better than they are? Do I think I deserve the blessing more?* If the answer is yes, you might need to do some repenting yourself!

SATAN'S LIE:
YOU ARE BETTER THAN THE
PERSON SITTING NEXT TO YOU.
#THEGRACESPACE

By thinking that his little brother did not deserve the feast, the excitement, and the grace, the elder brother was mischaracterizing the father. He thought that his father would be willing to *condemn* a son who came from his own loins, who repented, who asked for a place again in the father's household. The younger brother's *restoration* gave the older brother a *revelation* of the father's heart. He learned that it's not the beginning of the thing, it's the end. God never judges us by how we start out, but how we end.

And another thing. The elder brother was not the only witness to the father's indecent excitement over his son's return. You think that no one saw him hitch up his robes and sprint down the hill? The whole community had a front-row seat to the return of the prodigal son! They even got to join in on the festivities. The effect of the father's love spread to them all because they all knew the law. They knew how the son should be treated for dishonoring his father. And yet, they witnessed an amazing restoration which lead them to a greater understanding, revelation, of the mercy of God. He's not a God afar off. He is merciful. He is a God who runs to restore.

What the elder brother failed to realize is that his younger brother's sin did not take away his significance. I'm here to tell you today that your sin has not removed your significance. Every time we condemn someone else we are removing their significance. Every time someone condemns you they are unknowingly taking away your significance. Brothers and sisters, we are all significant before the Lord! There is equality in the grace that He has given each one of us!

GRACE DOESN'T KNOCK, IT KICKS THE DOOR DOWN.

How many times have we seen famous pastors or religious leaders fall on their faces in scandal and disgrace? And yet even when we get it wrong, God's Word is still true. His promises are not predicated on our responses. What's so radical about the grace of God is that it doesn't need permission from your failures to invade your situation and manifest God's Spirit like never before. Grace doesn't knock, it kicks the door down. Grace says, there's too much invested here to let this one go!

And later, like the prodigal son, you'll have the context to look back and say, *by grace* I have been saved!

The Spirit of Grace

Of how much sorer punishment, suppose you, shall he be thought worthy, who has trodden under foot the Son of God, and has counted the blood of the covenant, wherewith he was sanctified, an unholy thing, and has done despite to the Spirit of grace? (Hebrews 10:29)

The Bible refers to the Holy Spirit as the *"Spirit of grace."* In my opinion that would insinuate that the Holy Spirit is in the business of revealing the lovingkindness of the Father. If we are truly being Spirit-led, then we must make the Father's business our business. Too many Christians are in the business of tearing down rather than building up. Too many Christians are harboring wounds, hurts, and disappointments in the heart. These burdens weigh down their spiritual life. These devices keep people from enjoying the abundant life in its fullness. These are the tools that Satan uses to rip the church apart! But I thank God that the Word of the Lord says that He will build His church, and the gates of hell will not prevail against it. (See Matthew 16:18.) Once we embrace an attitude of grace, we will begin to experience a greater manifestation of the power of God in our lives.

I encourage you to consciously develop a grace space in your life and in your heart. This is a place where you allow the goodness of God to permeate everything that you think and do. This is a place where you choose to show love rather than condemnation. Grace is not weakness, it is the greatest strength. If only the older brother knew that by forgiving his younger brother he was in fact honoring his father, his thoughts and actions would've been totally different. Don't make the same mistake!

For Discussion

1. Dr. Bridges said that we often judge others according to their *actions* and judge ourselves according to our *intentions*. What would it look like in your life to flip those two around?

2. Why does living in community with other believers, attending church and other functions, force us to confront the wounds in our hearts? Would you say that isolating yourself as a Christian is unhealthy?

3. What does the parable of the prodigal son tell us about our heavenly Father? What can we learn from the elder brother?

Testimony

Years ago, I joined a social media prayer group. It was such a blessing. In my zeal and enthusiasm, I began to post specific testimonies of people being healed from terminal illnesses. Apparently, that wasn't the purpose of the group, because one of the group members asked me to take the testimony down. In their mind, the group was only for prayer requests. I was confused and a bit offended by the situation. However, instead of reacting in anger, I humbled myself and apologized for the misunderstanding. Later on, one of the members of the group corrected this person and said that their actions were inappropriate. The person reached out and apologized, and we were able to move past it. It was just a small instance, but instead of becoming offended, I extended grace, and it paid off.   —Sylvia

Prayer

Father, in the name of Jesus I thank You for the truth of Your Word. Your Word is a lamp unto my feet and a light unto my path. Thank You, Lord, for giving me a revelation of biblical grace. Your Word says that we should come boldly to the throne of grace that we may obtain mercy and find grace to help in time of need. I thank You for Your unmerited favor and Your supernatural power working in my life. I choose to release every person who is indebted to me or who has trespassed against me. I choose to walk by faith and not by my feelings. Thank You, Lord, for giving me a spirit of grace and compassion. In the name of Jesus!

Amen.

12

BE NOT DECEIVED

Be not deceived: evil communications corrupt good manners.
(1 Corinthians 15:33)

Throughout this book, we have discussed the plan of the enemy to steal, kill, and destroy people and relationships. We have uncovered his clandestine attack against the body of Christ in the form of slander, gossip, and offense. We have also discussed the fact that many Christians are unaware that they are now or have been at some time complicit in his attacks against the church. In this chapter, I want to focus on one of the most important components of our discussion: communication.

By *communication* I am referring to the means of connection between people or places. At the end of the day, we must realize that we were created to love and connect with people deeply. Everything we do and say as it relates to other people is extremely important. The Bible tells us in 1 Corinthians 15:33, *"Be not deceived: evil communications corrupt good manners."* Who and what you enter into fellowship, communion, and companionship with will ultimately affect your character. It is childish of us to think that we can listen to slander and gossip and not be affected by it. Every time we entertain evil, our character is inevitably corrupted, and it ultimately affects our ability to connect to community in a healthy way.

Have you ever heard something negative or deplorable about someone and attempted to have a normal interaction with that person as if you hadn't heard a single thing? It's impossible! Our *communion* is always affected by the *communication* we receive.

The Common Union

Every Sunday in our church in Tampa, Florida, we partake of Holy Communion, or as many call it, the Lord's Supper. We believe that there are very powerful spiritual benefits to consuming the Lord's Supper on a regular or semi-regular basis. We have witnessed amazing miracles as people have taken the Communion in faith, believing God to release His supernatural power in their lives. My own wife was physically healed while taking Communion, and we have seen and witnessed countless others experience similar healings. Why is Communion so powerful? What is the spiritual significance of Communion? We know from the Word of God that Jesus celebrated the Passover the same night in which He was betrayed, saying,

> *Take, eat: this is My body, which is broken for you: this do in remembrance of Me. After the same manner also He took the cup, when He had supped, saying, This cup is the new testament in My blood: this do you, as often as you drink it, in remembrance of Me.*
>
> (1 Corinthians 11:24–25)

As a Torah-observing Jew, Jesus was doing that which was required of every man by consuming the Passover Seder, but as the Son of God and Messiah of Israel, He was fulfilling Messianic prophecy by becoming the sacrificial Lamb that caused death to pass over us by the shedding of His precious blood. This is a very holy and powerful moment every time we observe it. However, there is more to Communion than our spiritual healing and redemption. Communion also represents the unity that should always be present and prevalent in the church.

Remember when we said earlier that God hates division because it goes against His Being of unity and love in the Trinity? Well, when we observe Communion, it represents that spiritual *union* between Christ and the church and between the people in the church. This is a *common* union between every person in the body of Christ, regardless of ethnicity, nationality, or gender. We become one in the Spirit. (See Ephesians 4:4.) I often tell my congregation that Communion is a perfect time to release people from all offenses you have held against them. This is a time for healing and restoration. How can we say that we love and adore God while we are holding a grudge against our brother or sister in Christ? We are called to unity!

Let Us Examine Ourselves

There is another very powerful component to the Lord's Supper that most people don't think about but which is vital to our discussion on slander and gossip. The Bible tells us:

Wherefore whosoever shall eat this bread, and drink this cup of the Lord, unworthily, shall be guilty of the body and blood of the Lord. But let a man examine himself, and so let him eat of that bread, and drink of that cup. For he that eats and drinks unworthily, eats and drinks damnation to himself, not discerning the Lord's body.

(1 Corinthians 11:27–29)

I want you to consider the fact that we are all members of the body of Christ. Every believer, man, woman, boy, and girl, constitutes the *ekklesia*, the church, the body of our Lord Jesus. Paul admonishes the church not to take the Communion unworthily, or in other words, irreverently or in an unfit manner. What does this really mean? To take Communion without a reverence and an appreciation for the people of God is to spite to the sacrifice of Christ Himself.

Is it really that serious? Yes! The term *"examine himself"* comes from the Greek word *dokimazō*, which means: to test, examine, prove, scrutinize, to see whether a thing is genuine or not. In other words, we must examine our hearts to make sure that we are walking in purity. Many times this is taught from the perspective of repenting of our personal sins, but it goes much deeper than this. It is also instructing us not to have a negative view of the body of Christ.

Can you imagine telling a man that you like him a lot but you hate his wife? Can you imagine telling a friend that you love their head but you hate their body? Can you imagine telling a parent that they might be great but their kids are brats? That is exactly what we are doing when we say that we love Jesus but can't stand the church. That is what we are saying when we pray to God in holiness but criticize, accuse, and condemn the body of Christ. The Bible says that if we do this we are *"not discerning"* the Lord's body. In other words, an attitude of anger, bitterness, or resentment toward your brother or sister in Christ is neglecting to recognize the deep value and significance they hold in the sight of God. It often leads to weakness and sickness within the church. This is why so many Christians are bound by physical and spiritual infirmities, because they don't recognize (or rightly discern) the truth that Jesus died for the people they often despise. This is a very serious issue! We must be intentional in our relationships with our fellow brothers and sisters in Christ, with the understanding that Jesus shed His blood to bring us into union with Himself *and* with each other.

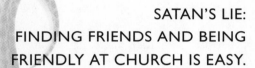

SATAN'S LIE:
FINDING FRIENDS AND BEING
FRIENDLY AT CHURCH IS EASY.
#BENOTDECEIVED

Relationship Stewarding

However, we must understand that unity is often a fight against ourselves. Are you willing to do what it takes to maintain harmony?

Contrary to popular opinion, relationships don't just happen—they require stewardship. In fact, relationships inside the church sometimes require *more* stewardship. I know it seems to be an oxymoron that people inside the church can be harder to get along with. And certainly you may have a wonderful experience of clicking right away with people inside the church and watching your relationships effortlessly grow into a beautiful friendships with backyard barbeques and Sunday morning prayer times. But I'm telling you, that is the exception, not the rule!

Remember back in chapter 9 when we talked about the heart being deceitful above all things? Those are *our* hearts we're talking about. Romans 3:23 says, *"For all have sinned, and come short of the glory of God."* What is a

Christian but someone who has been convicted by the Holy Spirit and has come before God, saying that same thing, "I have sinned, but I am resting in Christ! Forgive me and fill me and guide me!" None of us should be surprised that the church, filled with sinful people, has trouble getting along! The real question is what to do about it. And the answer is *stewardship*.

Stewardship means spending time with one another and honoring others during that time. Without investing time and being intentional about honoring those you are in relationship with, relationships will deteriorate and often end prematurely. The currency of relationship is time and the commodity of relationship is honor. Stewarding is one of the least developed skills in the church.

Don't blame the devil for a lack of proper stewardship! I find that people who always cry betrayal and offense in relationships are usually the main offenders. A friend must show himself or herself friendly. If you want better relationships, invest in being a better friend. Are you an instrument of unity or divisions? Do you help draw people closer together or do you push them further apart? Again I say, we must endeavor to keep the unity of the Spirit in the bond of peace.

Many people allow themselves to fall into deception in this area of their life. They grow offended, they feel betrayed, and by so doing they allow the enemy to keep them at odds with their brothers and sisters in Christ. This is not the will of God, beloved!

The Power of Self-Deception

The apostle James tells us something really powerful about self-deception:

> *But be you doers of the word, and not hearers only, deceiving your own selves. For if any be a hearer of the word, and not a doer, he is like to a man beholding his natural face in a glass: for he beholds himself, and goes his way, and immediately forgets what manner of man he was. But whoso looks into the perfect law of liberty, and continues therein, he being not a forgetful hearer, but a doer of the work, this man shall be blessed in his deed.* (James 1:22–25)

Every time I preach at my church, I make the people recite this confession: "The Word is my mirror; it's how I check myself. And what this mirror shows me is the truth. I am what it says I am! I have what it says I have! I can do what it says I can do!" Why do I encourage people to make this statement? It helps us to understand the importance of "look[ing] into the perfect law of liberty." Many people don't realize that the Word of God is the perfect mirror. You can absolutely trust everything it reveals to and about you.

But if we only hear the Word and don't do what it says, we deceive ourselves. We look into that mirror, shrug, and walk away thinking, *that mirror has problems.* We convince ourselves that what we *feel* is more important than what God *says.*

Let's say a person is hurt or wounded in a church setting, and, instead of doing what the Bible commands them to do and addressing the person directly, they choose to follow their emotions, avoid confrontation, and indulge in bitterness and offense. Even though they have just disobeyed the Word of God, they tell themselves that they are still in God's will. This is self-deception. Anyone who thinks they can harbor bitterness in their heart or walk in offense and still live a peaceful life is absolutely deceived.

THE DECISION TO FOLLOW WHAT WE *FEEL* RATHER THAN DO WHAT GOD *SAYS* ALWAYS LEADS TO SELF-DECEPTION.

I can remember a particular person in our church years ago who told us that they felt led by God to leave the church. We have a policy of blessing and releasing those who transition to another place or ministry, but we try to make sure there are no unresolved offenses. They assured us that there was nothing wrong and they were leaving only because God was "moving them out!" as they put it. Now I should mention that earlier I had corrected them for doing something wrong, and shortly thereafter they said God was telling them to leave. After they left, they broke fellowship with most people in the church and never contacted us. We have had many people who leave the church and return or at least visit from time to time. My assumption of this couple is that they would have kept some sort of relationship—unless they were offended! So why did they say they weren't? Self-deception! They looked into the mirror and saw bitterness in their hearts, but, by leaving the church, they totally skirted the problem instead of addressing it.

I cannot tell you how many times I have counseled people who say that they have forgiven everyone and that they are not keeping malice with anyone, yet they can't even speak to the person who hurt them. They have spiritualized their own bitterness and resentment so that it feels ok, but it is certainly holding them in bondage. In order to be free they must be willing to obey the truth. It is not enough to *hear* the truth, we must *know* and *obey* the truth in order to experience lasting freedom.

Pastors are not immune to this self-deception—far from it. No pastor is perfect, and we all need the humility to ask ourselves daily whether we are deceiving ourselves.

What's Your Narrative?

Earlier, we talked about the fact that offense is the bait of Satan. It starts with an enticement or seduction which ultimately leads to an entrapment, and most people do not realize they are trapped until it is too late. Why don't people recognize it quickly enough? Because of something I call an internal narrative. *Narrative* is defined as a spoken or written account of connected events, a story. Everybody has an internal narrative, the story that they tell themselves about what has happened, what should have happened, what could have happened.

What's your narrative? What's your story? This is one of the most important aspects of living in freedom from offense! The narrative you tell yourself will determine the outcome of the situation. The story affects the glory! Who is taking your glory?

Many people's internal narrative is misconstrued. In other words, they interpret the actions or words of others wrongly, leading to misunderstanding and ultimately offense. I cannot tell you the countless times people have misinterpreted my actions and vice versa. Someone came up to me once and asked why we didn't want them in church. I was so puzzled it was almost laughable! I thought to myself, *is this a joke?* I called my wife to come and be a witness to the conversation. I looked them in their eyes and said, "We never told you that!" They had such a confused look on their face at this point. Finally, they admitted that they had never *heard* it but that it was certainly *implied*. It would be an oversimplification to attribute this to dishonesty. I believe that many people assume that their perception is correct. I often joke that when people have a disagreement in the church and narrate the account, it's exaggerated to the level of an 80s action movie complete with armored tanks, grenades, and yes—Mel Gibson and Danny Glover!

ALL OF US HAVE A NARRATIVE;
WE HAVE A STORY WE TELL OURSELVES.

This is where the Holy Spirit comes in. The Bible refers to Him as the Spirit of truth. (See John 16:13.) We must allow the Holy Spirit to search our hearts and give us the right perspective, to take away the exaggeration and bias, and to open our eyes so we can see what's really going on.

I remember a particular instance where I was narrating a story and the Holy Spirit spoke to me and said, "It didn't happen like that!" In the quietness of my heart, I reflected back on the events in question and realized that my perspective was off.

Many times people tell themselves that the church is responsible for their hurt. I'm not talking about somebody in an abusive church who left it for many good reasons. I'm talking about somebody who tells me that all twenty churches they have attended have misunderstood, rejected, and wounded them. I remember a lady coming to our church claiming that no other church would allow her to walk in her gifting. According to her, they didn't embrace the prophetic gifting! It wasn't long before she left our church with the same grievance, even though our church embraces the gifts of the Spirit in their fullness. What happened? How could every church they had ever attended been the problem? If everywhere you go smells bad, it may be time to do some personal inventory. We must allow for the possibility of our own error. When we do, it keeps us from the pride that snatches at every bait the devil offers.

The Root of Bitterness

Years ago, I heard a sermon in which my pastor taught on "The Root of Bitterness." He took the phrase from this verse:

> *Looking diligently lest any man fail of the grace of God; lest any root of bitterness springing up trouble you, and thereby many be defiled.*
>
> (Hebrews 12:15)

I have found that many Christians are harboring a root of bitterness in their hearts. A root of bitterness is an area where seeds of rejection, hurt, or offense started growing underground where we thought they were hidden, but are now poking out above the ground and producing corrupt fruit. How do you know if there is a root of bitterness in your life? Here are a few signs:

1. Engaging in slanderous, negative, or toxic conversations about people or situations.

2. Recalling negative or hurtful events with crystal clarity.

3. Twisting or distorting Scriptures to justify negative emotions or anger toward others. (For example: "I discern that their spirit isn't right!")

4. Engaging in avoidance or other isolating behavior in an effort to reject or retaliate against the person who hurt you. This is also referred to as "cutting people off."

5. Building a case in your mind against the person(s) who rejected or hurt you.

6. Becoming defensive when someone is mentioned or crafting a self-narrative that accuses others and exonerates yourself.

**IF EVERYWHERE YOU GO SMELLS BAD,
IT MAY BE TIME TO DO SOME PERSONAL INVENTORY.**

The passage in Hebrews says that we should be *"looking diligently"* so as not to fail the grace of God, and not allow a root of bitterness to "spring up and trouble you." What we allow into our hearts will always "spring up!" The problem with a root of bitterness is that it does not just defile you, but also everyone you are connected to. It is time to lay the axe to the root of bitterness in your life. How do you do this? You must forgive all those who have hurt or offended you. See chapter 15 for biblical guidance on seeking healing.

Seeing Through the Matrix

One of my favorite movies of all time is the post-apocalyptic film *The Matrix*. In it, artificial intelligence is at war with humanity and has created a vast dream world called "the matrix" that most of mankind is plugged into, living ordinary lives inside their heads, all fabricated by the machines to keep them in the dark about reality. Almost everyone is duped. But the main character, Neo, is delivered and told the truth. In the third movie of this trilogy, Neo confronts a man possessed by his arch-nemesis, Agent Smith. In a very intense scene, Neo fights this possessed guy and loses his physical eyesight—but is able to see Agent Smith inside his opponent. Despite his blindness, Neo says to Agent Smith, "I can see you!"

SATAN'S LIE:
IF THERE ARE HYPOCRITES
IN CHURCH, YOU SHOULD LEAVE.
#BENOTDECEIVED

God is raising up a generation of believers who, like Neo, will be able to see through the matrix of offense, hurt, anger, and bitterness, and realize that behind it all stands the enemy of their soul. Satan is keeping many believers in a deceptive dream world. He is the hidden perpetrator working behind the veil of human flesh and human emotions, seeking to keep the body of Christ bound and afflicted. Be not deceived!

Once you open your eyes to the truth, the power of deception is broken. But you can't open your eyes until the Word of God illuminates your life. This is why meditating on and obeying the Word of God is of utmost importance. Until now, you may have felt trapped in "the matrix." You may have wondered if you could ever be free or lead a peaceful and prosperous life. The good news is that you can experience lasting freedom. You don't have to be offended anymore.

In the book of Ephesians, we're told that we do not wrestle against flesh and blood, but against principalities and powers, against the rulers of the darkness of this world. (See Ephesians 6:12.) The word *darkness* there is the Greek word *skotos*, which literally means ignorance or spiritual blindness. In other words, Satan's scheme is to keep you and me in the dark. He doesn't want us to know what he is doing. He wants us to believe that the church is our enemy and not himself.

I have even heard countless people say that they don't go to church because of all the hypocrisy. This is deception! Would you stop going to work because of slackers? Would you stop going to the gym because of overweight people? Absolutely not! Requiring that type of perfection from the church is unnatural; the church is exactly where the hypocrites should be, so that they might learn to cast aside their hypocrisy.

Satan does not want you to realize the deception. He wants you to isolate yourself from the church. The enemy is very clandestine, he uses people and they don't even realize how they have been sub-contractors for the kingdom of darkness! He doesn't come with horns, pitchforks, or flames breathing out of his nose. He hides behind slander, false accusations, gossip, hatred, anger, abuse, offense, bitterness, and jealousy.

When we accentuate the faults in others, we ignore our own. You may have experienced hurt by someone in the church, but this is no excuse for breaking fellowship with the body of Christ.

GOD'S WORD HAS THE POWER TO LIBERATE US FROM DECEPTION IN ANY AREA OF OUR LIVES.

For Discussion

1. What is Communion, or the Lord's Supper, a picture of? How can it help us understand our role in church?

2. What are the six fruits of the root of bitterness? Have you seen any of these fruits in your life?

3. "The currency of relationship is time and the commodity of relationship is honor." Does this ring true with your experience? Why or why not?

Practicum

1. Does your church need a grace space? How can you grow a grace space in your church and your home? Pray toward that end.

2. Everybody has an internal narrative, the story that they tell themselves about what has happened and what should have happened. What's your narrative? Find someone you trust, and talk through what your internal narrative is toward believers and the church. Declare the presence of the Spirit of truth in your heart and in your conversation. (See John 16:13.)

3. Do you sometimes feel trapped in a matrix—in a prison of misunderstanding? Break free through declaring the power of 2 Corinthians 3:16–18.

Testimony

I struggled with offense for many years. It wasn't from the standpoint of "they are out to get me," but rather "they don't like me because I'm not likeable." I was offended at *myself* and I constantly accused myself, which caused me to easily become offended and therefore accuse other people. Most of the time, I had no idea I was operating out of offense. When I felt that I was being left out, told off, or unjustly bossed around, I didn't speak up. Refusing to go to the source of my upset feelings, I instead came up with reasons and scenarios in my own head for why things were the way they were. My fear of confrontation, of rebuttal, of rejection, and of retaliation led me to harbor offense in my heart toward others.

I didn't start becoming free from offense until I decided to confront the issues of my heart head on, both within myself and with the people who I felt had wronged me or who I had wronged. I learned that it wouldn't just go away if I acknowledged it to myself and then worked hard to "forget about it." I had to speak up and tell my sister or brother in Christ, "I feel like this because…," and allow them the opportunity to address my concerns. Communication and honesty have helped me to experience freedom from offense. Though I still come up against many situations that can cause me to be offended, I am now able to tell myself, "that shouldn't even bother you" or to talk it out with the person, and then genuinely move on.   —*Anonymous*

Prayer

Father, in the name of Your Son, Jesus, I thank You for the power of Your Holy Spirit. The Holy Spirit is the Spirit of truth; therefore, I walk in truth in every area of my life. Lord, Your Word declares that we are one body. I recognize that You are the God of unity. Therefore, I choose to walk in unity with my brothers and sisters in Christ. I refuse to participate in strife or division. I know that this is displeasing to You. Instead, I choose to be a vessel of healing, wholeness, and unity. Father, I ask that You reveal any area of deception in my life. Right now, I lay the axe to any root of bitterness in my heart. Father, I thank You that I walk in the light of Your truth continually. In the name of Jesus.

Amen!

13

THE LAW OF HONOR

Children, obey your parents in the Lord: for this is right. Honor your father and mother; (which is the first commandment with promise;) that it may be well with you, and you may live long on the earth.

(Ephesians 6:1–3)

The Lord has shown me over the years the absolutely vital importance of the law of honor. God revealed it to me while I was reading a very popular story in the Bible: the story of Noah and his three sons, Shem, Ham, and Japheth. Noah had these three sons when he was five hundred years old. Talk about vitality! After the flood, when Noah proved himself to be a faithful man of God, he also proved to all of us that there is nobody perfect—no, not one! One day he got drunk and staggered to his room. When his middle son found him, Noah was passed out on the floor, naked. The Bible tells us that Ham left the room and the next thing we know Shem and Japheth are walking into it. The Bible says that they never looked on the nakedness of their father. Instead, they backed into the room and covered him with the sheet.

When Noah awoke from his drunken state, his first order of business was to curse his middle son's children. The Bible says that Noah decreed: *"Cursed be Canaan; a servant of servants shall he be to his brethren"*

(Genesis 9:25). We know from biblical history that Ham was the father of the Canaanites. The question is, why would Noah utter such a terrible curse? What was so serious about what Ham did?

It was then that God gave me a revelation. Ham violated a spiritual law. He looked upon the nakedness of his father. He showed no respect. Spiritually speaking, it is the child's responsibility to cover the father. Our fathers give us instruction, they teach us the ways of God, and they cover us physically; in exchange, we are required by God to cover them spiritually. This is a spiritual prototype of honor.

Honoring Our Natural and Spiritual Parents

If there is one thing that the Western church lacks tremendously, it would have to be honor. I am not saying that there is no honor in the church today, but I am saying that there needs to be more.

To honor is to esteem highly and attach significance to someone. It is actually the same word in Hebrew that is also translated *glory*. The Bible tells us to honor our fathers and mothers in the Lord. I have often heard it debated whether or not we should have spiritual fathers and mothers. But according to Ephesians 6, this is a spiritual principle. Just as we have natural or biological fathers and mothers, we also have spiritual fathers and mothers. These people can be those who raised us in the gospel, or they can be those who adopted us and helped us to develop in our spiritual lives.

I thank God for my spiritual father because he helped to disciple me in the things of God and to grow me into the man that I am today. Along with my biological father, he is responsible for the success that God has produced in my life. I am not suggesting that he takes the place of God or gets the credit for what God has done, but I *am* acknowledging that he is a vital part of my development. This is so important for the church to understand.

Unfortunately, like Ham in the Bible, many people have uncovered the nakedness of those whom God had given as spiritual oversight in their lives. Ham saw his father's weaknesses, and his first reaction was to tell his brothers. God was not pleased with this. It was a violation of spiritual protocol. The test of true spiritual maturity is not how we handle the strengths of others but how we handle their weaknesses. Until we can properly handle the weaknesses of our spiritual fathers, we are not qualified to be sons and daughters. Do you talk about your leaders or do you pray for them? Can you be trusted to see their weaknesses and not to run and tell your brothers and sisters? Instead, will you cover them in intercession and grace?

Just as children dishonor their natural parents, in the same manner many Christians dishonor those in spiritual leadership. Every time you gossip about and criticize your pastor, you are dishonoring him or her. Every time you put yourself on equal footing with your spiritual leader, you are operating in dishonor.

The truth is, no leader is perfect. Yes, I know that sounds like profanity, but it is true! Every person that God will ever use to speak into your life and to develop your character has flaws. Often, God allows you to see their flaws so that you can develop your character in the area of their weakness, or so that you can be of a help to them. As a result of Ham's transgression, his children had to pay the price of dishonor. What we honor appreciates in value and what we dishonor depreciates. There are countless people in the church who wonder why their lives are not thriving and fruitful— yet they have never embraced the spiritual law of honor. What would happen if they tried?

But do you know why I have a great relationship with my pastor today? It's because I was willing to stick with him through the offenses. I perceived things that were hurtful and, even, debilitating. However, because I recognized that my responsibility to honor God was greater than my right to be upset, God was able to bring me out of physical, emotional, and spiritual difficulty into the situations and circumstances ordained for my life. What God has for you is greater than what you're going through right now.

Now I want to take a minute to clarify something. There are times when fathers and mothers abuse their children, both in the physical and in the spiritual realm. I am not suggesting that people remain in abusive situations. When you are in danger, are suffering from physical pain, feel constantly ashamed and humiliated, have friends who are concerned about you, or show any other symptoms of abuse, seek help and please remember that the most loving thing to do to an abuser is to turn them in to the proper authorities! That is a huge subject that I am not qualified to tackle, but please hear me when I say that abuse is serious, it happens, and it can never be condoned. We will talk about how to recognize spiritual abuse in a later chapter.

Mature Emotions

Remember, disagreement is not the same as dishonor. We have the option of disagreement, but we do not have the option of dishonor. You might say, "But they were wrong!" Yes, they may very well have been wrong! God will deal with His servants, but the moment you take it upon yourself to stand in the judgment seat, you will stand to be judged. Let us honor our leaders! To do anything else is a sign of immature emotions.

Today we live in a culture where disagreement is thought to be a license for dishonor. For example, the way we speak about our president or our vice president or other elected officials is often deplorable. Even Christians have adopted the practice of dishonoring those in positions of authority. Beloved, the Bible strictly prohibits this kind of behavior:

> *Let every soul be subject to the higher powers. For there is no power but of God: the powers that be are ordained of God. Whosoever therefore resists the power, resists the ordinance of God: and they that resist shall receive to themselves damnation.* (Romans 13:1–2)

This might seem like a tall order. But let me remind you who the *"higher power"* was at the time when the apostle Paul penned these words: Emperor Nero. Nero is still infamous for his abuse of Christians and his terrible rule over the Roman Empire. It's even possible that he set the city of Rome on fire—and then blamed Christians for it![3] And yet Paul says, *"Let every soul be subject to the higher powers."*

One time when I was in a ministry, it was my turn to lead worship with my worship team, but I arrived late to practice. One of the leaders over the worship team came up to us and said, "You all are not leading worship today!" They already had a whole other rehearsal going. I was thinking, *What in the world? It's our turn!* I had pride in my heart and I wanted to retaliate. I walked right up to the leader and said, "I'm off the worship team."

Now those words were spoken out of an angry emotion, out of pride. And I was wrong to say them. Because the worship was never about me

---

3. See https://www.britannica.com/biography/Nero-Roman-emperor.

to begin with; it was about Jesus! When you're in a church and you're under a leader, a leader has a right to tell you to "sit down" every now and again. You need to observe the admonition and sit yourself down until God says otherwise. When you don't act out of obedience, you will be premature in your actions, not mature.

The reason why I had to go through seasons where my pastor would sit me down, where he wouldn't acknowledge my wishes, where he wouldn't do the things I wanted him to do—those were the times that God was trying to mature my emotions. If you get into ministry, you can't have emotions that are immature. You can't have emotions that are premature. You have to learn how to step back. You have to learn how to sit down, to marinate, to wait on God. You have to learn how not to vindicate yourself. You've got to learn how avoid the trap of being embroiled in feelings and emotions. You have to learn how to get in that space with God, and say to Him, like Moses did, "Speak to me…if you don't go before me, I'm not going!" (See Exodus 33:15.)

That is discipline. That is a choice. That is what mature emotions look like.

**SATAN'S LIE:
REBELLION IS
A SIGN OF STRENGTH.**

#THELAWOFHONOR

Pride and Rebellion

The irony is that many of the people who fall victim to the subtle trap of pride and rebellion are very kind-hearted and loving. Remember, Satan was not always Satan; he was once known as Lucifer, a beautiful cherub in heaven. It was iniquity in his heart that transformed him into something vile and deplorable. In the same way, people usually do not start off in rebellion against God, but when they do not deal with offense properly, it causes them to become something other than what God originally intended.

What do we mean when we speak of pride and rebellion? Well, pride is simply a vain concentration on self above God. When we are operating in pride, we often focus on our feelings and emotions above the Word of God. Rebellion is a refusal to submit to God's way of doing things or a resistance of biblically sanctioned authority. These two work hand in hand. It is always pride that motivates rebellion. For instance, a person may have experienced a painful or offensive situation in church, and as a result, they say within himself or herself, "I will never submit to a pastor again!" Even though this may seem justified emotionally, it goes directly against the Word of God.

I can remember a situation in which a lovely couple came to our church. They were personable and helpful. They always offered to meet the needs of the church. On top of all of this, they were huge givers. Yet there was something missing. I noticed that they would never receive from anyone else. It was as if their giving became a mechanism to keep them from having to subject themselves to anyone else, including the leadership. Though they were helpful and kind, they were not submitted to the leadership of the church. The evidence was the fact that they always wanted to be in charge or in control of whatever they were doing. The moment they were corrected about a wrong action, they were immediately offended and eventually left the church. Why? The church had wounded this precious couple in the past, and as a result, they accepted the lie from the enemy that the only way they could be safe was to be in control, and the only way to be in control was to be in charge. Right? Wrong! Though they loved God and had a desire to serve Him, they were operating in a spirit of hurt, pride, and rebellion.

Anytime we are harboring offense in our heart, it will distort our reality. We will interpret correction as rejection, and control as protection. The truth is, our safety can only be secured when God is in control. We will only walk in true freedom when we are submitted to His ways and not our own.

Your Pastor Is Not Your Peer

The reason why people are so easily offended by spiritual leaders is because they believe that they are on the *same level* with their leader, and people are generally less willing to take rebuke, criticism, or other offense from their peer. But God does not introduce the Christian life as a free-for-all where anyone can hate on whomever they want. Rather, He instituted the roles of leaders in the church.

Here in the United States, we pride ourselves on our democracy, our system of government by all eligible citizens through elected representatives. A democracy suggests that the people put the leaders in power and therefore, the leaders are accountable to those who elected them. If we don't like the law of the land, we have the freedom to peacefully lobby to change the laws.

Many treat the kingdom of God in the same way. However, the kingdom is not a democracy! It is a theocracy, meaning that God is at the head. God establishes the law, and He is the One who appoints His representatives to exercise authority over the people.

SATAN'S LIE:
YOUR PASTOR IS YOUR PEER.
#THELAWOFHONOR

I am not suggesting that pastors should run the government, but I am saying that, from a spiritual standpoint, God puts the church leadership in charge of the church. Most Christians don't really see things this way. In many denominations, pastors are hired just like a person is hired in the secular world. And if a person can be hired, they can also be fired. Now, there are certainly legitimate grounds for the removal of a person from leadership, but we are not our leaders' employer! Leaders are not beholden to us, and they are not our buddy that we hang out with one weekend and ignore the next! The Bible says: *"Obey them that have the rule over you, and submit yourselves: for they watch for your souls, as they that must give account, that they may do it with joy, and not with grief: for that is unprofitable for you"* (Hebrews 13:17).

Your pastor is not your peer! Your pastor is the one who has been given spiritual oversight of your soul and should be treated with the utmost respect and honor. Why? Because God is holding them responsible for you! *"They must give account."* In the same way that God holds those responsible who cause a child to stumble, He holds the church leaders responsible for the watching over of the souls of the sheep. It is a mutually beneficial community, where all watch for the good of each other. But it disintegrates when there is no honor.

I know that this concept may not be popular, but it is definitely biblical. If you don't know what it means to honor your spiritual leader, then ask God to show you what it means. And to really walk a path of discovery, ask the spiritual leaders in your life about what it means to honor them.

Worthy of Double Honor

Let the elders that rule well be counted worthy of double honor, especially they who labor in the word and doctrine. (1 Timothy 5:17)

The reality is that God respects the office and the function of the minister, and holds it in high esteem (even when the minister doesn't). The church is not a democracy, nor is it a rotary club. Though we are all one in Christ, when it comes to ministry and leadership, there is a difference between the sheep and the shepherd.

HONOR IS THE SYPHON OF THE SUPERNATURAL.

In a world of social media and smartphones, ministers are easily accessible and relational, but this does not diminish their value or exempt believers from the biblical command to honor those in a position of authority. When we honor our leaders, we are honoring God and positioning ourselves to receive the prophet's reward: *"He that receives you receives Me, and he that receives Me receives Him that sent Me. He that receives a prophet in the name of a prophet shall receive a prophet's reward"* (Matthew 10:40–41). I often tell people that honor is the syphon of the supernatural. Through honor we access the grace that God has placed on those entrusted to lead us. In this age of hypercriticism, we must endeavor to create a culture of honor in our homes and churches, where spiritual leaders are valued, celebrated, and appreciated. Never speak ill of your spiritual leader or use your words to tear him or her down. This is a grievous offense in the eyes of God.

Through the grace of God, we have managed to develop a very specific culture of honor in our church. People value and appreciate spiritual leadership and one another. There is a particular couple in our church that I want to use as an example of honor and humility (though there are many that I could use to illustrate this truth). Any time I am traveling out of the country or intercontinentally, this couple will sow a significant financial seed into my life. Whenever they see a nice item of clothing in the store, they will pick up something for my wife. Oftentimes, they don't even tell us that they are going to do these things; it is just sporadic and spontaneous. On one occasion, this couple came to me and thanked me for speaking into their life and for praying for their family. I released a blessing over them.

As time went on, one of their children got into some very serious trouble with the law and was facing jail time. We prayed for her to have an abundance of favor in the courtroom. When it was time for the family to stand before the judge, he looked at them and said, "There is something different about you! I am throwing the case out." Praise God! This is the reward of honor. When we honor those God has placed in authority over us, we open the door to the blessing and favor of God.

The Curse of Dishonor

Just as there are tangible rewards for honoring those in spiritual authority over us, there are consequences for operating in dishonor. Please don't misunderstand me; I am not suggesting that a leader has a right to curse anyone in their church or anywhere else, but I am saying that God will hold us accountable for speaking against or dishonoring those whom He has set over us: "*Whoso curses his father or his mother, his lamp shall be put out in **obscure darkness**"* (Proverbs 20:20). I have heard this passage of Scripture referred to as the "20–20 Vision Scripture": if you want to have clear spiritual vision, this is the Scripture that you must always remember. Earlier, we spoke about curses—imprecations of evil spoken out of our mouths concerning someone else. Curses can also be the spiritual consequence of violating God's laws. Just as there are consequences for dishonoring our biological parents, there are consequences for dishonoring our spiritual parents.

I have seen this narrative play out time and time again in my own life, but it's also present in Scripture. Remember Miriam? The Bible says that she spoke against Moses (her younger brother) and her hand became leprous. Even though Moses was Miriam's younger brother, he was also her spiritual leader. And it's not just some ominous, Old Testament concept—Ananias and Sapphira were New Testament believers who lied in the presence of the Holy Spirit and died instantly. (See Acts 5:1–11.) A friend of mine once told me that he spoke against his pastor to other people, and the next day his body was literally racked with pain. He could hardly get out of the bed! As he began to pray, the Lord spoke to him saying, "Touch not My anointed and do My prophets no harm!" (See Psalm 105:15.) He immediately repented of his dishonor and the Lord healed his body.

SATAN'S LIE:
SUBMISSION TO AUTHORITY IS
FOR WIMPS AND CHUMPS.
#THELAWOFHONOR

"Caution: No Life Guard on Duty"

There was a subdivision near my childhood home that had a really nice pool. The pool was for residents only, but we had friends who lived in the neighborhood so we were allowed to swim in the pool as their guests. Near the pool was a white sign with huge red letters that read: "CAUTION: No Life Guard on Duty." In other words, we had to swim at our own risk. There was no one there to catch us or rescue us if we fell into the deep end.

The same is true when it comes to the law of honor. Anytime a person speaks against someone in spiritual leadership, they are swimming at their own risk. Many Christians are swimming in the deep end of the pool without a life jacket or flotation device. Eventually, they will end up drowning if they are not careful. God will never help you to go against one of His own. It is an exercise in futility and can lead to your own demise. I remember a person coming to our church and speaking negative words about me to one of the other members. They said that I was a charlatan who made up fake miracles and that it was not possible to operate in the power of God the way I claimed. The next day, the person went completely deaf in both ears. I was asked to pray for them to receive their hearing, and I prayed for them accordingly. They immediately received their hearing! Clearly, this was an example of people who couldn't swim who had veered off into the deep end. Make sure you are not going into territory that God says is off-limits.

> **COUNTLESS BELIEVERS ARE DROWNING IN A POOL OF PAIN, REGRET, AND DESPAIR ALL BECAUSE THEY OPEN THEIR MOUTHS AND SAID SOMETHING THEY HAD NO BUSINESS SAYING.**

The Bible says, *"Touch not My anointed, and do My prophets no harm"* (Psalm 105:15). This Scripture has been abused by many and been twisted and used as justification for some terrible things, but its application is still true. I have said before and I will say again; you may not like or agree with the person, but you have an obligation to respect and honor the office they hold. If only the church would catch this revelation, we would stay out of so much trouble! When we choose to operate in dishonor, it reflects poorly on the kingdom of God as a whole.

Have you experienced the heartache of a parent when a son or daughter refuses to speak to or acknowledge them? And yet people behave this way in the church every Sunday. If you walked in a church and everyone seemed to have a negative attitude of the pastor, would you go back to that church? Why not? Because their house is not united, and a church of disunity is a church of danger. On the other hand, if there was a church where everyone walked in love toward each other and showed the utmost respect for leadership, you would want to go back and experience it again. We must develop a culture of honor, not dishonor!

For Discussion

1. What can we learn about the law of honor from the story of Noah and his three sons?

2. Have you ever been specifically told what to do by someone in spiritual leadership? Was it difficult? How did you respond?

3. Where in our society today do we see disrespect for authority? Where do we see respect?

Testimony

I was attending church with and living with one of my relatives for a time. One night we got into a very heated argument and began to exchange hurtful and offensive words. It almost ended up in a physical altercation. The truth was that this had been brewing for some time because I constantly felt demeaned and disrespected by her. Once the argument began that night, all the visceral emotions came to the surface. I was asked to leave. I was so hurt and angry, I didn't know what to do.

Then I heard the Holy the Spirit say, "Forgive!" I thought, "How could I forgive someone who has shown me no respect?" Again, the Holy Spirit said, "Forgive!" Finally, I released the person. The next time I saw her in church, I went and apologized for my actions even though I felt I was the one wronged. She apologized to me as well. Something broke in my heart and I felt a release. We were able to forgive and be reconciled. I decided to not allow the enemy to win.

I have learned that sometimes it is better to take the wrong. To God be glory! Today we are back in fellowship with each other and have moved passed the offense.

—*Anonymous*

Prayer

Father, in the name of Jesus, I thank You for Your unconditional love toward me. Lord, I ask You to teach me how to honor those You have placed in leadership over me. As You teach me the law of honor, I will continually honor those whom You have called. Whether I agree with them or not, I still choose to honor them. I declare that as I so honor, I will also reap honor. Your Word says to touch not Your anointed nor do Your prophets any harm; therefore, I refuse to use my mouth to attack men and women of God. I recognize that such is the plan of the enemy, and I refuse to participate in his plan. I declare that everything I do is covered in honor and integrity, in the name of Jesus.

Amen.

|4
MY BROTHER'S KEEPER

For this is the message that you heard from the beginning, that we should love one another. Not as Cain, who was of that wicked one, and slew his brother. And wherefore slew he him? Because his own works were evil, and his brother's righteous. (1 John 3:11–12)

I have no doubt that the vast majority of Christians know that we must love one another. We embrace it theologically. We even embrace it doctrinally. However, it is a totally different thing to walk in love *practically* in our relationships with other people. I am thoroughly convinced that if the church would get a better understanding of what real love looks like, we would be much less prone to offenses.

We have, as a biblical example, an interesting character named Cain. He was Eve's firstborn son. After Eve gave birth to Cain, she had a second son named Abel. The Bible tells us that Cain was a tiller of the ground, whereas Abel was responsible for the livestock. One day, Cain offered the fruit of the ground as an offering unto the Lord and Abel offered the first of the flock as an offering unto God. The Lord respected Abel's offering but rejected Cain's. The Bible tells us that in his intense anger, Cain killed his brother Abel.

God knew what Cain had done, and He asked him, *"Where is Abel your brother?"* Cain infamously responded, *"Am I my brother's keeper?"* (Genesis 4:9). Why would Cain make such a statement? The truth is, he knew that what he had done was evil, but he was hiding under the guise that he owed no responsibility to his brother. His disdain demonstrates what goes wrong when we think we have no responsibility to the brothers and sisters next to us. Cain's response begs the question, are we our brother's keeper? The answer is a resolute *yes!* And if we refuse that responsibility, it is as if we slay them.

SATAN'S LIE: THE CHRISTIAN LIFE IS EVERY MAN FOR HIMSELF.
#MYBROTHERSKEEPER

His Blood Is Thicker than Water

Have you ever heard the term, "Blood is thicker than water"? This colloquial expression means that the bond between family is stronger than the bond between everyone else. Let me ask you a question: if someone spoke evil of your biological brother with whom you're very close, what would you say to them? Would you celebrate the negative statements? Would you share it with others as juicy gossip? No! You would probably be very upset that someone would have the audacity to speak against your blood brother that way. Why? Because he is your brother! That fact alone is enough to protect the relationship. Yet we speak evil of our sisters and brothers in the body of Christ every single day. It seems that deep down we don't really believe that they are our brothers and sisters.

However, in the eyes of God, the bond between fellow believers is stronger than the bond between biological siblings. In fact, Jesus shed His blood to make us one family. Jesus prayed a profound prayer in the gospel of John: *"Holy Father, keep through Your own name those whom You have given Me, that they may be one, as We are"* (John 17:11). The entire spirit of the New Testament hinges upon love and unity.

This issue of strife and division is further exacerbated by the fact that we live in a society that tells us we are not the same. Blacks are pitted against whites; rich are pitted against poor; men are pitted against women. This is not the will of God. God sees us as members of one body, with unique functions and gifts inside the church. (See Romans 12:5–6). As long as we refuse to acknowledge the fact that we are one, we will continue to perpetuate the devil's evil scheme as it relates to slander and gossip in the church.

The Curse of Cain

Why did Cain kill his brother? The simple answer is that he was jealous, but what if there were more to it than that? Isn't it ironic to consider that Eve lost her inheritance in the garden of Eden by succumbing to temptation, and that her son then suffered a similar fate? He was banished from fellowship with his family as a result of the sin of murder:

And the LORD said to Cain, Where is Abel your brother? And he said, I know not: am I my brother's keeper? And He said, What have you done? the voice of your brother's blood cries to Me from the ground. And now are you cursed from the earth, which has opened its mouth to receive your brother's blood from your hand; when you till the ground, it shall not hereafter yield to its strength; a fugitive and a vagabond shall you be in the earth. (Genesis 4:9–12)

God cursed Cain, and said that the ground would not yield its strength. In other words, he would no longer be able to enjoy a fruitful life. He was bound to a life of barrenness. Many believers have adopted the same fate as Cain. As a result of the bitterness and offense that they consistently walk in, their lives are unable to produce lasting fruit. They are like spiritual fugitives running from place to place and from church to church, seeking refuge. Unfortunately, many churches are aiding and abetting fugitives. They join the choir at your church after they have assassinated the character of every choir member at their former church. They gush over your pastor and assassinate the character of their former pastor. They love on your nursery and assassinate the characters of the nursery helpers at their former church.

Whenever I meet a person who seems very interested in joining our ministry and their story doesn't quite add up, I ask them who or what they are running from. Many people are running from the past. They connect to new things and people in an attempt to hide from the old, but this is not God's way. While it is true that every situation cannot be resolved the way we might like, we must make sure that we are doing everything God has required of us and seeking to keep the unity of the Spirit in the bond of peace. (See Ephesians 4:13.)

Earlier, we talked about the vagabond spirit. People who harbor offense and bitterness often become spiritual vagabonds and fugitives. They stay away from intimate relationships. They rarely ever connect to spiritual communities. Rejection leads to offense, offense leads to bitterness, and bitterness leads to hatred. The key to breaking this cycle of pain is repentance. If you notice, Cain never repented for his wrong. When confronted with his sin, his response was, *"Am I my brother's keeper?"* Not "Lord, forgive me!" His heart was hardened to the fact that God held him responsible for the well-being of his brother. God will hold us responsible for each other, too! Don't harden your heart.

Confess Your Faults

The Bible tells us, *"Confess your faults one to another, and pray one for another, that you may be healed. The effectual fervent prayer of a righteous man avails much"* (James 5:16). Most people don't realize that the church was designed to be a safe haven for the hurting. Many people don't know this because the church, by and large, has not portrayed herself in this manner in recent years. Instead of being a safe haven for the lost, many churches have been prison cells for the bound. Many people have been their brother's killer (in a spiritual sense) rather than their brother's keeper. We talk of raising the dead while we practice killing the living.

WE TALK OF RAISING THE DEAD WHILE WE PRACTICE KILLING THE LIVING.

This is not what Jesus had in mind when He shed His precious blood for the church. He desires a place of hope, healing, and restoration. How do we become that place of healing He desires? We must forgive each other and begin to see one another as brother and sister and not enemies.

We are members one of another. (See Romans 12:5.) The Bible tells us that we should confess our failures and faults to one another and pray for one other, so that we can experience healing.

This has often been misinterpreted to mean that we should confess our sins to someone else in order receive *forgiveness*, but that's not what the verse says. The word used is *healing*. There should be a safe and trustworthy atmosphere in the church where we can share our shortcomings and our challenges with mature brothers and sisters in Christ who will help us to experience healing and wholeness in that area.

Wherever there is gossip and slander, it is, of course, very difficult to be honest and vulnerable. People are uncertain whether what they share will be held in confidence or not. Ironically, sometimes the people who complain about gossip and slander the most are the main perpetrators. The only way to create an environment of trust is to be trustworthy. You must give what you desire to receive.

Love Covers a Multitude

Earlier we talked about the parable of the prodigal son, a perfect illustration of our Father God's heart. The simple truth found in that story is that *love covers*. Too many of us have embraced a philosophy of exposing rather than covering. Every time we gossip or slander; we are exposing people's faults and flaws. Again, this is not the same as biblical rebuke. If you are spreading private matters about a friend to a third party, you are not helping him or her at all; you are hurting. The Bible says: *"Hatred stirs up strifes: but love covers all sins"* (Proverbs 10:12). And, *"He that covers a transgression seeks love; but he that repeats a matter separates very friends"* (Proverbs 17:9). The word *cover* here means to conceal or clothe.

You may be wondering why we should seek to cover other people's sins. Simple! Jesus covered your sins! The only reason we can approach the Father without guilt and shame is because we have been cloaked in the righteousness of Christ.

When I became a parent, this principle became abundantly clear to me. One day, one of my children came to me to report that their sibling disobeyed. They were very proud of themselves. I asked them how I should discipline their sibling, and they said that I should spank them.

I said I would gladly oblige, with one condition: I would have to spank *them* as well. All of sudden the punishment seemed too severe to my child. I asked them why, and they told me that they didn't do anything wrong. I told my child that they did do something wrong; they exposed the other sibling with pride in their heart.

Now, I believe that it is important to understand that there are times when we have to tell someone else about a particular situation, especially when it involves a person doing harm to another or to themselves, but this is different from exposing someone else for our own self-interest. Like my child running to me to tattle-tale, we often want to see people exposed or embarrassed for what they have done, forgetting that God doesn't deal with us like that, but rather deals with us in love and forgiveness.

SATAN'S LIE:
IT'S NOT YOUR FAULT
YOU CAN'T KEEP SECRETS!
#MYBROTHERSKEEPER

God Covers to Restore

I want you to imagine that someone hurt himself or herself physically and the injury left a gaping wound. What is the first thing that you would do? Emergency aid tells us that we must first cover the wound and stop the bleeding. Why is this important? First of all, to prevent the excessive loss of blood which could lead to a more severe condition or even death. Second, to prevent the wound from becoming infected. The purpose of concealing the wound is to facilitate further healing.

The same is true spiritually. As a pastor, I have found that many situations have been resolved and healed when we endeavored to correct the person in private and to cover them in love. This is not always possible in a conventional sense, but we can always make a conscious effort to cover a brother and sister. Covering means extending grace. Covering means maintaining dignity. Covering means exemplifying compassion. I am not always commanded to agree with you, but I am commanded to cover you.

When a government agent sells secrets to a foreign government it's called espionage. This is actually a form of treason. When was the last time that someone told you privately that they had a struggle or problem in their life and you went and told someone else? This is not pleasing to the Lord. Can you imagine going to a pastor for a counseling session and then hearing everything that you discussed in private coming from the pulpit as a sermon illustration the next Sunday? You would probably feel awful and never come back! Yet people do this every day in their interpersonal relationships.

Beloved, God only exposes what He intends to correct and heal. Let us be keepers of each other's souls and cover each other in grace.

Overcoming Betrayal

If I have not been transparent enough, let me just say: I have gone through more betrayal in ministry than I have in any other time of my life. I have been lied about, back-stabbed, manipulated, slandered, and the worst part is that it has been executed by people whom I have dearly loved and have supported on a regular basis.

Some of the deepest pain that we will ever experience is in the church because the church represents God. It is a place where we express our worship and adoration of the Lord. It is a place of fellowship and community. Sometimes we feel more peace in the church that we feel in our own homes. So when we are hurt by the church, it is a deep and visceral thing.

What do you do when the place that represents healing hurts you the most? How do you move forward when you have experienced spiritual abuse? What should be our reaction when we experience betrayal?

Jesus was our spiritual prototype, demonstrating the Father's plan for us to walk in freedom and peace. His own disciple betrayed Jesus into the hands of sinners. Can you imagine how painful this must have been? Yet He never once stepped outside of His character. Many think that this was easy for Him since He was divine, but I would beg to differ. The Bible is very clear: *"For even hereto were you called: because Christ also suffered for us, leaving us an example, that you should follow His steps"* (1 Peter 2:21). Christ is our example, which means it is possible to forgive and show love regardless of what has been done to us. Maybe your spouse has betrayed your trust. Maybe a fellow brother or sister in Christ has spoken lies about you. Maybe a son or a daughter has rejected you. Maybe a pastor has exploited a private conversation. Regardless of who or what has caused you pain—Jesus is the answer. Just as He carried our betrayal, so He gives us the strength to carry others' betrayal.

I once counseled a particular pastor who was spiritually and emotionally burnt out. His overseeing pastor had promised him that he would be promoted to a senior pastor role within his organization, and yet, when the time came for him to ascend into the new position, the overseeing pastor changed his mind. He was absolutely devastated! He felt hurt and betrayed.

EVERY TIME WE FACE BETRAYAL, WE HAVE A CHOICE WHETHER TO BE BITTER OR TO BE BETTER.

Like this pastor, many people seem to receive the "short end of the stick" at times. Betrayal is a very real part of ministry. When people whom you trusted disappoint you or walk out of your life (seemingly prematurely), it can be devastating. I have had people who promised me, "I'll be with you to the end!" walk away when I needed them the most. However, God always wants us to put our trust in Him and not idolize the people around us. Even Jesus Himself underwent deep betrayal, but was able to overcome it because He always placed His trust in the Father.

This doesn't mean that we are to be suspicious or distrustful of people, but it means that our eyes and hearts are to remain focused on Him, not each other. Through every betrayal that I experienced, God took me to a place of greater power, influence, and compassion because at some point I was willing to let go and trust Him. Jesus knew that Judas would betray Him, but He never focused on the betrayal. Instead, the Bible says: *"Looking to Jesus the author and finisher of our faith; who for the joy that was set before Him endured the cross, despising the shame, and is set down at the right hand of the throne of God"* (Hebrews 12:2). Jesus knew that His eternal reward was of greater substance than His present pain; therefore, He endured the cross, despising the shame. Don't worry, this doesn't mean that you have to be crucified, but it does mean that you must be willing to let go and let God. The greatest form of betrayal is when we betray our assignment on account of offense. Stay faithful to your assignment, just as Jesus stayed focused on His!

The Spirit of Apostasy

Speaking of betrayal, it is important to understand the spiritual climate in which we live, and what it means for the church today. The Bible admonishes us, *"Now the Spirit speaks expressly, that in the latter times some shall depart from the faith, giving heed to seducing spirits, and doctrines of devils"* (1 Timothy 4:1).

Have you ever wondered how so many people could be deceived in the last days? Or consider this even more disconcerting reality: a great deal of this deception will manifest itself in the church, of all places! When we think of apostasy we often think of the extreme falling away of believers in the end times, but apostasy can and will be more subtle than that. I believe that the spirit of apostasy is alive and well and that it desires to spread throughout the body of Christ today, right this minute. It is not waiting for the end times.

Peter denied the Lord three times, after promising Him that he would die for Him. In most cases people never intend to betray anyone; they simply succumb to a spirit of betrayal. What do I mean by this statement? Anytime we put our own self-interest above that of others we are bound to betray someone or something. Peter never fathomed that he, of all people, would betray Jesus. However, in the heat of the moment, he was attacked with fear and put his own safety above loyalty to his beloved Teacher. I do not say this to excuse betrayal in any way, but it helps to give you a different perspective.

Jesus warned us, *"And the brother shall deliver up the brother to death, and the father the child: and the children shall rise up against their parents, and cause them to be put to death"* (Matthew 10:21). The spirit of betrayal is very real, but we can guard our hearts and minds against this sinister weapon of Satan by dealing with our own hurts and offering forgiveness, not offense. Remember, hurt people tend to hurt others. This is more than just an emotional tendency; it is a spiritual reality.

We must guard our hearts against this spirit of apostasy and deception. We must embrace the disciplines of prayer, fasting, and spiritual commitment. Too many in the church have been double-minded, serving the God of comfort and convenience rather than the God of our Lord Jesus Christ who has called us to sacrifice and self-surrender.

NEVER ALLOW THE BETRAYAL OF OTHERS TO CAUSE YOU TO ADOPT AN ATTITUDE OF DISLOYALTY.

Self-Evaluation of the Spirit of Apostasy

Are you aiding and abetting a spirit of apostasy in your life?

Here are a few questions to ask yourself:

1. Am I committed to a local body of believers in covenant relationship? Am I part of a healthy, Bible-based local church?

If so, what is your role and responsibility to this community? Being a part of a godly assembly of believers is a key component of warding off deception.

2. Have I learned to commit to the things of God despite difficulty and challenges?

If you never learn to commit to the basic things of God (that is, prayer, discipleship, and studying the Word), how can you be trusted with greater things? The spirit of apostasy will certainly operate in the vacuum of a lack of commitment.

3. Are you willing to suffer for righteousness' sake in order to honor God's Word?

Regardless of the growing perversion and deception in society today, God's Word has never changed and neither should you when it comes to morality and truth.

Once we take inventory of our hearts, we can determine whether we are being faithful to the truth of God's Word or defecting to another doctrine. The biggest lesson that the Lord has taught me through betrayal is faithfulness. Continue to love those who may not extend the same love toward you. The Lord will reward your faithfulness.

For Discussion

1. What does the story of Cain and Abel teach us about our relationships with each other?

2. How is the devil using the disunity all around us today to divide the church? How can we fight it?

3. Have you ever been betrayed by someone who was close to you, whom you trusted? Did this chapter change your perspective on that betrayal in any way?

Practicum

1. Pray about lending support to the spiritual leaders in your life. Ask God to reveal to you what support they might need: An encouraging word? A financial blessing? Someone to fix their kitchen sink? Act on it, remembering that so *your days may be long upon the land which the LORD your God gives you* (Exodus 20:12).

2. Can you be trusted as a safe haven for other believers, or do you suffer from "run and tell it" disease? Can God use you as an instrument in someone else's healing and restoration? If you are harboring offense toward someone, go to him or her and seek reconciliation. Pray for one another and watch God begin to bring healing to your heart.

3. Loyalty is directly related to support and trust because a loyal person offers support and can be trusted, among many other positive things. Make of list of the areas in your life where you want to become more loyal, whether they are relationships, attitudes, organizations, or any other area. Pray to God for the strength and resolve to be disciplined in your loyalty in those specific areas.

Testimony

I had been a pastor for twenty years when my closest spiritual son betrayed my trust and broke away to start his own church without my knowledge or blessing. There were many in my church that followed him, including some of my most active and loyal members. This was devastating for the entire church, but it took a serious toll on me in particular. I must admit that I was very bitter about the situation. The situation not only affected me spiritually, but also emotionally and physically. It affected my blood pressure, my heart, and my weight. Eventually, I decided to release the person who betrayed me. It was not an easy thing to do, but the Holy Spirit helped me to forgive. Today by grace I have forgiven, my health has improved, and I am finally free. —*Bob*

Prayer

Father, in the name of Jesus, I thank You for the compassion and grace that You have demonstrated toward me. You delight in mercy. I thank You for Your mercy and Your unfailing love toward me. Lord, I recognize that I am my brother's keeper; therefore I choose not to expose my brothers and sisters in the Lord. Instead, I choose to cover them with grace. Lord, just as You have covered me, I choose to cover them. Thank You for giving me a revelation of the significance of the body of Christ. In the name of Jesus, I pray.

Amen!

15

WHEN CHURCH HURTS

And they that shall be of you shall build the old waste places: you shall raise up the foundations of many generations; and you shall be called, the repairer of the breach, the restorer of paths to dwell in.

(Isaiah 58:12)

In all that we have shared so far there is a recurring theme: God is in the business of restoration. Almost every person whom God used in the Bible had experienced supernatural restoration at some point in their lives. I believe the same is true for you and me. Maybe you have been deeply hurt by the church. Maybe you have been warned about someone in leadership. Maybe you have been the victim of slander or gossip. No matter where you are or what you have been through, God desires to restore you today.

I know what it's like to walk through pain. This book was not birthed out of some theological pondering or philosophical exercise. This book was birthed out of my own struggles and the revelations that God gave me in the midst of them. I know what it's like to be told by leadership that you will never succeed. I know the frustration of being lied to and maliciously talked about. I also know what it's like to experience deep betrayal. If I can be honest, I have probably perpetrated some of these things against others.

Let me tell you a story I heard once of a grandfather and his two granddaughters. The two granddaughters were playing with crayons. They both wanted the yellow one, and in their squabble over it, the crayon broke into little pieces. The younger one was beside herself and ran to her grandpa with the broken crayon, crying, "She broke the crayon! She broke it, she broke it!" In his wisdom, the grandfather took his granddaughter's hand, picked up the crayon, started tracing it on paper, and said, "Look, sweetheart, broken pieces still color!"

YOUR PAIN WILL NEVER NULLIFY YOUR PURPOSE.
YOU ARE SIGNIFICANT, VALUABLE, AND LOVED.

You might feel broken today. You might be disillusioned with the church. You may even be afraid to connect with community. I want you to understand today that broken pieces still color. Despite all of the things that you have been through, you have not lost your value, your significance, or your purpose.

In fact, I believe that God is going to use you as a repairer of the breach. In Isaiah 58, the Bible tells us that we will build up old waste places and raise up the foundation of many generations, and we will be called the repairers of the breach. God has called us to restore broken foundations. He has anointed us to bring healing to the brokenhearted. If you have been wounded, hurt, or offended, you are a candidate to be an instrument of restoration in the life of someone else.

The Potter's House

You may have heard the story of the potter's house before, from the book of Jeremiah, but it's worth another listen. And if you've never heard it, listen up!

Arise, and go down to the potter's house, and there I will cause you to hear My words. Then I went down to the potter's house, and, behold, he wrought a work on the wheels. And the vessel that he made of clay

was marred in the hand of the potter: so he made it again another
vessel, as seemed good to the potter to make it. Then the word of the
LORD came to me, saying, O house of Israel, cannot I do with you as
this potter? says the LORD. Behold, as the clay is in the potter's hand,
so are you in My hand, O house of Israel.   (Jeremiah 18:2–6)

Though this story is given within the context of ancient Israel and
their sin, we can extract a powerful application for the church today. Just
as it was a prophetic picture of the house of Israel, it is a prophetic picture
of the church today.

God wanted Jeremiah to go down to the potter's house. There He
drew his attention to a piece of clay that was on the potter's wheel.
Jeremiah noticed that the clay was marred. And yet the potter used the
wheel to restore the clay back to the shape he desired.

SATAN'S LIE:
YOU'RE TOO BROKEN
TO BE IN CHURCH.
#WHENCHURCHHURTS

Many of you reading this book have been marred by hurts, pains,
and disappointments. You may have wondered, *Where is my place in the*
body of Christ? God is asking you a profound question today: "Cannot I
do with you as this potter does to his clay?" Just as the clay was in the
potter's hand, so are you in the hand of the Most High God. If you will
allow Him, He will bring a level of restoration to your heart and soul that
you never fathomed possible.

The Church Needs You

If you believe, you are part of the body of Christ. And if you are part
of the body of Christ, *you are needed!* Don't take my word for it—it's all
over the New Testament. Paul stresses again and again, every believer
is needed. In other words, the church needs you: "*So we, being many, are*
one body in Christ, and every one members one of another" (Romans 12:5).

If your toe is severed, then your body can't walk! If your eyes are shut, then your body can't feed itself! Your whole body is in jeopardy if one little part does not work. Anybody who would tell you that you don't have a role in church or that you don't need church is contradicting the Bible! Paul is clear that the church needs us and we need church.

SATAN'S LIE:
YOU DON'T NEED CHURCH
TO BE A GOOD CHRISTIAN.
#WHENCHURCHHURTS

However painful it is, we are part of one another and the whole body needs each part:

For the body is not one member, but many. If the foot shall say, Because I am not the hand, I am not of the body; is it therefore not of the body? And if the ear shall say, Because I am not the eye, I am not of the body; is it therefore not of the body? If the whole body were an eye, where were the hearing? If the whole were hearing, where were the smelling? But now has God set the members every one of them in the body, as it has pleased Him. And if they were all one member, where were the body? But now are they many members, yet but one body. And the eye cannot say to the hand, I have no need of you: nor again the head to the feet, I have no need of you.

(1 Corinthians 12:14–21)

But I'm not saying that real and terrible hurt doesn't happen. What I call PTSD in the church is all too common.

PTSD: Pastoral Traumatic Stress Disorder

I'm sure you've heard of PTSD. According to the Anxiety and Depression Society Association of America, "Posttraumatic stress disorder, or PTSD, is a serious potentially debilitating condition that can occur in people who have experienced or witnessed a natural disaster, serious accident, terrorist incident, sudden death of a loved one, war, violent personal assault such as rape, or other life-threatening events."[4] People go to war or live through a horrific disaster, and it messes with their minds and their emotions for the rest of their lives.

I want to inform you that soldiers and those who witness natural disasters are not the only ones who experience the difficult, life-changing effects of a scene of trauma. Church members are suffering *spiritually* from the traumatic scenes happening within our very churches.

When congregants live through a terrible church split or disaster, it can mess with them spiritually for years. This is what I call Pastoral Traumatic Stress Disorder. It's a spiritual condition that takes place when the leadership or people within the church community traumatize a person. If you are suffering from this, you don't say "that's my pastor," when pointing him or her out to a friend. You say, "that's the pastor of my church." People who have experienced PTSD avoid developing authentic and intimate relationships within the church for fear of being hurt or betrayed again.

When a pastor is not living up to the standard of what a pastor should be, how do you get over that traumatic experience? I have ministered to thousands of people in the church who were wounded by spiritual leaders, and as result were unable to achieve victory in their spiritual lives. Some of them have permanently defected from the church. This is not the will of God. People are hurt when things go wrong. The key to recovery is deep repentance and inner healing. We must allow the Holy Spirit to administer the power of God in the areas of our deepest hurts and disappointments, for then and only then will we become productive members of the body of Christ.

The Difference Between Judging and Condemning

We talked about the importance of honoring our leaders. But how do we honor a leader who has failed us? Morally, spiritually, practically, *failed*. What should a church do then?

It's a complicated subject, but there are really one of two options: condemning or judging. They may sound the same, but they are not! The

4. "Understand the Facts: Posttraumatic Stress Disorder (PTSD)," Anxiety and Depression Association of America, updated June 2016, https://www.adaa.org/understanding-anxiety/posttraumatic-stress-disorder-ptsd, accessed October 7, 2016.

Bible says, *"Judge not, and you shall not be judged: condemn not, and you shall not be condemned: forgive, and you shall be forgiven"* (Luke 6:37). In the context of this passage, the word judge means "to pass judgment" on another person and the word *condemn* means "to pronounce guilty." While God instructs us in His Word to use discretion and discernment concerning right and wrong, He does not give us the right to "pass judgment" on others or sentence them to condemnation. Instead, we are called to be compassionate to those who fail or struggle in their flesh. Jesus was hard on the religious leaders, but was merciful toward the tax collectors and the publicans. Why? People are still valuable, even when they fail.

CONDEMNATION IS A DEAD END. BUT JUDGING GIVES A WAY FORWARD.

However, in other Bible passages, we are called to judge. *"Open your mouth, judge righteously, and plead the cause of the poor and needy"* (Proverbs 31:9). *"Do you not know that the saints shall judge the world? and if the world shall be judged by you, are you unworthy to judge the smallest matters? Know you not that we shall judge angels? how much more things that pertain to this life?"* (1 Corinthians 6:2–3). The judging in these passages is wisely determining a necessary course of action. It's a forward movement. Condemning, on the other hand, is a dead end, not a way forward. It's the last word. There is nothing to follow. Only God has the power to condemn! Yet He never condemns His children! Can you imagine that there are people willing to do to others what God is unwilling to do to them?

Judging (in a mature spiritual sense) is holding people, including ourselves, accountable. If, for example, I am in a situation where I am doing something wrong in the church, my wife, an extremely wise and discerning person, can help bring in a different perspective, and ultimately hold me accountable for my wrong viewpoint or my mistake. There must be sound and uncompromised judgment. I thank God for a wife who is extremely honest and objective, because it helps to keep me balanced.

However, it is also very healthy to have people outside my home who will hold me accountable, no matter what, and judge what I am doing. I need to be accountable before God, a vertical accountability, but it can't stop there. I need horizontal accountability, too. I need human beings who will look me in the eye and point me in the right direction. And my wife cannot be my only source of accountability because that is too heavy a burden to bear. For this reason, I willingly submit myself to fathers in the faith who will speak into my life and challenge me to honor the Word of God. In the multitude of counselors, there is safety. (See Proverbs 15:22.) There are several pastors and other leaders in my life who are permitted to ask me the tough questions, such as "How's your marriage?" or "How are you doing emotionally?" The reason leaders of all kinds are accountable to those above us is to be accountable to those under our leadership. If you are not accountable to the people above you, you're at the mercy of the people under you.

There's a huge difference between holding people accountable and condemning them. I can remember experiencing deep failure in my life. I felt ashamed and condemned. The weight of guilt and defeat was so heavy that I felt that I could not move forward. The enemy constantly reminded me of my failure and unworthiness. But God didn't take the opportunity to kick me while I was down, instead He reminded me of my true identity in Christ. He put mentors and spiritual fathers around me who gave me sound counsel. They corrected me, they rebuked me, and they loved on me. As a result of their faithfulness to God I was able to experience the restoring power of the Holy Spirit in that area of my life. I was judged, but not condemned.

Signs of Spiritual Abuse

What is spiritual abuse? Essentially, abuse is simply the improper use of someone or something. Spiritual abuse is a misuse of spiritual authority. Many times, people who are under spiritual abuse don't even recognize it. It was the late Dr. Myles Munroe who once said, "Where purpose is unknown, abuse is inevitable!"[5] It is important to understand the purpose and the intent of the church. Once you understand the purpose of the church, you can know what to expect from the church and its

5. Dr. Myles Munroe, *Understanding the Purpose and Power of Women* (New Kensington, PA: Whitaker House, 2001), 40.

spiritual leadership. The church is not a social club. The church is not a recreation center or a fashion show. It is a body of believers submitting to one another out of love and honor, for the sake of the spread of the gospel.

How do you know when you are in a spiritually abusive situation? When is it time to leave a church or organization? As a pastor and leader, I have seen dozens of cases of spiritual abuse in the church. I have also been the victim of spiritual abuse. I have observed several characteristics of a spiritually abusive church.

SATAN'S LIE: THE PASTOR'S WORD TRUMPS GOD'S WORD.
#WHENCHURCHHURTS

When a leader is manipulative or controlling, this is a sign that the atmosphere is not operating according to God's intent. I once had someone tell me that their former pastor would tell the church members the color and type of clothing to wear. This is absolutely ridiculous! When leadership is constantly demeaning and shaming the congregation in an effort to force them to behave in a certain manner, it is certainly a sign of spiritual abuse. If the leadership of the church is constantly encouraging you to engage in activity that directly violates the Word of God, then you can be sure that you are in a spiritually abusive situation.

Another sign of spiritual abuse is isolationism: in such a case, the pastor will tell the church members to disassociate themselves from family and friends. People will be told to no longer communicate with people who have left the church. The pastor is the only person who can preach, teach, or serve in any influential position within the church. Rebuke is harsh, cruel, and debilitating. Marriages and families are often torn apart by the church. You may not be allowed to visit other churches, and if you leave, you are verbally cursed from the pulpit.

Now, let me bring some balance to this discussion. There are many who claim to be victims of spiritual abuse whose claims are simply rebellious and divisive. I have seen this many times. They may have received biblical correction, but biblical correction is not the same as abuse. A sound pastor will bring loving correction from time to time, but a sound pastor will never cultivate a demeaning or chastising atmosphere. If you feel something like that every time you come to church and sense something disturbing about the church environment, I think you should pray about it and bring it to the attention of leadership. If a church is consistently violating the Word of God and perpetuating abuse, it may be time to gracefully and prayerfully transition to another church.

Abusive Sheep

There is an old adage, "Hurt people hurt people." Nothing could be truer! When people are hurt, they often become hurtful. The same is true of members in the church community. I have said before that sometimes sheep *bite*. What does a leader do when the people under his leadership become abusive? How do you recognize this type of abuse?

Well, we know that those in leadership have a responsibility to steward the flock accordingly, but the sheep also have a responsibility to respect, honor, and uphold the unity of the church. When sheep become excessively critical and demeaning of their spiritual leaders, this can also be a form of spiritual abuse. Sheep who constantly drain pastors of their time and energy and never show any appreciation or respect for their leader are emotionally abusing their pastor. They tell the pastor to come and cut their grass, change their light bulbs, and counsel their children, and yet they don't offer any support to the church or leader, spiritually or financially. There was a saying that I heard once, "Give us a pastor and we will keep him broke and humble."

Some people believe that the pastor is beholden to their every whim and opinion. They're always asking, "Why does the pastor drive that car? Why does the pastor live in that house? Why should the pastor wear such a nice suit?" Everything the pastor does is under their scrutiny and investigation.

I have seen churches hire pastors and treat them like children. Nothing the pastor does is good enough. I have even heard of deacon boards changing the locks on the church doors when the pastor no longer meets their criteria. Beloved, this is manipulation and control, and God is not pleased with it. These individuals need to recognize that they are operating in the flesh and not the Spirit. Abuse can flow both ways!

We Need an ICU in the Church

Although we all have the *capability* of abusing others, the flip side of the coin is that we all have the *responsibility* of peace-making. We all have the responsibility for reconciliation. At some point, we each one are wounded, and we need an ICU. Sometimes it's you. Sometimes it's me. Sometimes it's the pit of depression because you have sinned. Sometimes it's the pit of depression because you have been sinned against.

You know, it's interesting, God spent more of the Bible talking about the restoration than He ever talked about correction. In every prophetic book, God talked about chastisement but always with restoration attached. Everything in the New Testament leaves room for restoration. When we understand this, it gives us a better context for how to deal with those who have failed us, and those times when we fail ourselves. It also helps us to understand how to set up an ICU in the church!

> MANY LEADERS ARE BLEEDING,
> AND WE CONDEMN THEM FOR LEAVING
> BLOOD ON THE CARPETS!

I recently read a piece by a pastor that broke my heart. This man had been a successful pastor of a large church with a new book each year and a beautiful family. He was something of a celebrity in the Christian world. But in just a short season, things unraveled. Through personal and professional mistakes, he messed up in his ministry, resigned from his church, filed for a divorce, and essentially tried to withdraw from the public eye. Things got so bad that he was actually contemplating killing himself and wrote a suicide note.

This piece was intensely painful for me to read. I am not saying that he did not do wrong! But what we don't see is that by the time a pastor falls, there is so much that's happened before. Many leaders are bleeding, and we condemn them for leaving blood on the carpets! They are gravely sick, and we must never demonize or vilify the sick. In the depths of that darkness, why was there no one to minister to him? No one to come alongside him? We talk a lot about praying for people. Someone comes to us with a problem, and we say, "We'll be praying for you." But do we really?

WHY DO WE CONDEMN PEOPLE PUBLICLY FOR WHAT GOD FORGIVES PRIVATELY?

We must help each other! We must always remember that the perfect will of God is restoration. Unfortunately, the church has done a terrible job of restoring the fallen. The church has attempted to master discipline. But it has not mastered restoration. We are very good at exposing, but it is a totally different thing to bring healing and wholeness to the wounded. The Bible admonishes us:

> *Dare any of you, having a matter against another, go to law before the unjust, and not before the saints? Do you not know that the saints shall judge the world? and if the world shall be judged by you, are you unworthy to judge the smallest matters? Know you not that we shall judge angels? how much more things that pertain to this life? If then you have judgments of things pertaining to this life, set them to judge who are least esteemed in the church. I speak to your shame. Is it so, that there is not a wise man among you? no, not one that shall be able to judge between his brethren? But brother goes to law with brother, and that before the unbelievers.* (1 Corinthians 6:1–6)

Paul poses a profound question, "are you unworthy to judge the smallest matters?" The idea that we cannot handle matters on our own but have to involve the tabloids is despicable. By allowing our brothers and sisters to be tried in the court of public opinion, we are in essence abdicating our spiritual authority and relinquishing our spiritual influence to the world.

Restoration always happens in private. Why do we condemn people publicly for what God forgives privately? Pastors and leaders will continue to fall, and hard, unless we foster an atmosphere where they can be restored. Most of the time when pastors leave church, it is because they have been exposed. But can we provide an atmosphere where the fallen can expose their own failings? Even when our brother and sister falls, we need a spirit of meekness: "Brethren, if a man be overtaken in a fault, you which are spiritual, restore such a one in the spirit of meekness; considering yourself, lest you also be tempted" (Galatians 6:1). Let us pray for one another, especially our leaders; if and when they fall, let us bear them up! Let us find the wise ones among us to judge between us when needed, with the goal of restoration.

For Discussion

1. Is there a time to leave a community? If so, what are the signs? How can you tell when to leave? How can you leave a church in a godly way?

2. How do we maintain the dignity of the person who's fallen? How do we maintain our own dignity?

3. Why does church hurt so much, so often?

Testimony

I was deeply wounded by one of the leaders in the church. It was so debilitating that I left and stopped attending church for several years. After a very long time, I relocated to another city and there I found a church. I was reluctant at first, but I eventually attended and got involved. It was in this church that I learned to have a relationship with God. It was there that I finally found peace and was able to forgive the people who had wounded me in the past. Once I forgave, the hurt went away, and I was able to find true happiness and freedom.

—*Mr. Willis*

Prayer

Father, in the name of Jesus, I thank You for Your everlasting love. I recognize that Your love is unconditional. You do not look at me based upon my faults, but You look at me through the veil of the blood of Your Son, Jesus Christ. Therefore, I choose to look at other people through Your eyes. I know that You are the Potter and I am the clay. I give You full permission to mend me and mold me into the image that pleases You. Heal my broken heart. Restore every area in my life. I want to be whole again. In the name of Jesus.

Amen!

16
HEALING THE WOUNDS OF THE PAST

*But to you that fear My name shall the Sun of righteousness arise with **healing in His wings**; and you shall go forth, and grow up as calves of the stall.* (Malachi 4:2)

Her eyes were full of suspense; her heart was racing as she gazed upon this marvelous sight. *Is this real?* she wondered as the majestic, portentous voice pierced through her soul. *"Fear not,"* the voice proclaimed, *"for you have found favor with God. And, behold, you shall conceive in your womb, and bring forth a son, and shall call His name JESUS."*

How could this be? Mary thought. *What will my fiancé say?* Again the voice declared,

He shall be great, and shall be called the Son of the Highest: and the Lord God shall give to Him the throne of his father David: and he shall reign over the house of Jacob for ever; and of His kingdom there shall be no end. (Luke 1:30–33)

And so by a supernatural act of God, the Seed which would become the Christ was housed in the womb of Mary. He would deliver the people from their sins in fulfillment of the prophetic word given to the Serpent in the garden of Eden: *"And I will put enmity between you and the woman, and between your seed and her seed; it shall bruise your head, and you shall bruise his heel"* (Genesis 3:15). A Man-child would be born who would reverse the curse released upon Adam and Eve for their sin. Thousands of years later, the damage done by that old Serpent would be undone.

This is the story of redemption: the triumph of the Seed of the woman over the Serpent who seduced, deceived, and stole man's authority. This is the story of our wonderful Savior and Messiah, who gave His life so that we could be free. Everything about the story of redemption is a testament to God's grace, which enables us to find healing and redemption from the wounds of the past. Adam failed, but Christ (the second Adam) succeeded.

The purpose of this book has been to walk readers through a journey of healing and restoration from the debilitating wounds that have kept so many living beneath the life that God intends. I want to help people find out what God has called them to do and walk in the grace that enables them to fulfill that call. I also want to help people recognize that our true struggle is not with *people*, but with the Accuser of the brethren, who accuses us before God and to one another every single day. God desires to expose the lies of the enemy so that you and I can live in lasting freedom and victory.

Will You Be Made Whole?

If you remember in chapter 1, we discussed how Eve was bewitched by the slanderous words of the enemy; she allowed herself to be seduced and manipulated through a conversation that ultimately led to her spiritual death. Who would have thought that a conversation could cost so much? We discovered that it is the nature of Satan to slander and accuse the children of God, and to deprive believers of their abundant lives in Christ. Knowing these things, you and I have a very serious choice to make. Will we continue in our hurt, fear, pain, and ignorance, or will we allow the Holy Spirit to restore us completely?

In John 5, the Lord gives us a very powerful example of someone who experienced healing and wholeness:

*After this there was a feast of the Jews; and Jesus went up to Jerusalem. Now there is at Jerusalem by the sheep market a pool, which is called in the Hebrew tongue Bethesda, having five porches. In these lay a great multitude of impotent folk, of blind, halt, withered, waiting for the moving of the water. For an angel went down at a certain season into the pool, and troubled the water: whosoever then first after the troubling of the water stepped in was made whole of whatsoever disease he had. And a certain man was there, which had an infirmity thirty and eight years. When Jesus saw him lie, and knew that he had been now a long time in that case, He says to him, **Will you be made whole?** The impotent man answered Him, Sir, I have no man, when the water is troubled, to put me into the pool: but while I am coming, another steps down before me. Jesus says to him, Rise, take up your bed, and walk.* (John 5:1–8)

The man in this story was clearly broken and wounded, and had been in this condition for a very long time. Yet Jesus shows up on the scene, and everything changes. I want you to know that no matter how long you have been sick, wounded, or hurting, Jesus is the Healer! Jesus asked the invalid man a profound question: *"Will you be made whole?"* Why would He ask such a question? We might think, *of course the man wants to be whole again!* But the truth revealed here is that we must make a decision. Healing is a matter of our volition; we must *desire* to be healed.

HEALING IS A MATTER OF OUR VOLITION; WE MUST *DESIRE* TO BE HEALED.

As you might suspect, the man at the pool of Bethesda began to make excuses for his condition. He said that there was no one there to put him in the pool and everyone else got to the pool before him. In other words, his focus was still on what people had done to him. For thirty-eight years he had been wounded and offended by other religious people. No one was compassionate toward him. No one took out the time to understand his plight or offer him assistance. Yet Jesus stood in front of him and asked him the most empowering question of his life: *"Will you be made whole?"* I ask you the same question today: will *you* be made whole?

The next words uttered by our Lord are absolutely shocking! *"Rise, take up your bed, and walk!"* This was a command! This was an invitation! This was an empowerment! "To rise" literally means to awake from sleep or to arouse out of the slumber of death. This man was in a state of spiritual death. Jesus came to resurrect him from the dead. The phrase *"take up"* is the Greek word *airō*, which means to raise up, to elevate, or to appropriate. In other words, Jesus called him higher; He elevated his thinking. Jesus called him above and beyond the attitude of victimhood into an attitude of victory. Finally, Jesus told the man at the pool of Bethesda to walk. This is the Greek word *peripateō*, which means: to move forward, progress, and regulate one's life. Jesus told him to move forward. He empowered this man to walk out God's purpose for his life.

Jesus is calling you and me to rise, take up our bed, and walk. No longer will we lie by the pool of self-pity, waiting for God to move in our lives: He is moving right now! Today is your day of healing, deliverance, restoration, and wholeness!

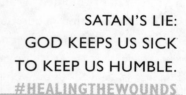

**SATAN'S LIE:
GOD KEEPS US SICK
TO KEEP US HUMBLE.**
#HEALINGTHEWOUNDS

Go and Sin No More!

The question remains, why was he in this condition to begin with? This is very important in our discussion about wholeness and healing, because once we discover the root cause of this man's affliction, it will help us to stay free.

Every time I read this story, I always focus on the healing of the man at the pool. But if we only focus on the healing, we miss another very important part of this story. In the fourteenth verse, Jesus finds the man in the temple. The Bible says: *"Afterward Jesus finds him in the temple, and said to him, Behold, you are made whole: sin no more, lest a worse thing come to you"* (John 5:14).

Remember, the man had been unable to walk—had been bed-ridden—for over thirty-eight years. I would've thought that Jesus would say something like, "Hey, it sure is great to see you up and walking around!" Instead, Jesus tells the man to sin no more so that a worse thing won't come upon him. Why? In biblical hermeneutics there is something that we call implied biblical interpretation. The implication in this particular text is that it was the man's sin that made him an invalid. He was not born that way. Not only did his sin put him in that condition, but his attitude *kept* him in that condition. This is why Jesus confronted his mind-set. He told him to remember where he came from. Jesus wanted him to understand the value of his wholeness so that he would never revert.

Many believers have been incapacitated through offense and bitterness. Like this man at the pool of Bethesda, they have found themselves unable to move and to function in the things of God. The Lord wants us to live in wholeness. He wants us to walk in our purpose. This can only be achieved when we refuse to participate in things that lead to bondage and brokenness. You have a decision to make: walk in freedom or live chained to a chair. The choice is yours! We must refuse to participate in slander and gossip, because these things do not foster wholeness.

IT IS ONLY THE SICK PERSON WHO SLANDERS; THE WHOLE PERSON SPEAKS LIFE.

Have you ever noticed that Jesus healed this man for the purpose that he would testify about the Christ? In verse 13, we read that he did not know who this man was who had healed him because Jesus had left to avoid the crowds. Later, when Jesus finds him in the temple and says, *"Behold you are made whole: sin no more, lest a worse thing come to you,"* the man felt the wholeness of his *spiritual* self, not just his physical self, and suddenly knows that this Man must be God. The next verse reads, *"The man departed, and told the Jews that it was Jesus, which had made him whole"* (John 5:15).

When we are made whole and experience the forgiveness of Christ, we, too, cannot help but recognize that spiritual healing can come only through God—and we witness to His holy Presence, telling everybody around us about what He did. That is the sign of a believer made whole, of a church made whole. They use their mouths to testify to Christ, like Mary, instead of heeding gossip and participating in slander, like Eve.

Healing the Broken Heart

In the book of Luke, the Bible records:

And he came to Nazareth, where He had been brought up: and, as His custom was, He went into the synagogue on the sabbath day, and stood up for to read. And there was delivered to Him the book of the prophet Isaiah. And when He had opened the book, He found the place where it was written, The Spirit of the Lord is upon Me, because He has anointed Me to preach the gospel to the poor; He has sent me to heal the brokenhearted, to preach deliverance to the captives, and recovering of sight to the blind, to set at liberty them that are bruised, to preach the acceptable year of the Lord.

(Luke 4:16–19)

SATAN'S LIE:
FORGIVENESS DEPENDS ON
THE OTHER PERSON
#HEALINGTHEWOUNDS

Jesus was anointed by the Father to heal the brokenhearted (among other things) and to proclaim the acceptable year of the Lord. Has your heart been broken? Have you experienced the pain of betrayal? If the answer is yes, then you are a candidate for healing. The good news is that God wants you to be whole. He longs to restore you in every area of your life.

Maybe you have been the victim of slander or gossip. Maybe you have been abused within the church setting. Maybe you have slandered others. No matter what your situation is, the remedy remains the same. You must forgive. You must forgive others and you must forgive yourself.

This is the only way to receive the anointing that destroys every yoke and lifts every burden in your life. This is not theoretical for me; I am speaking from personal experience. The Lord healed me of church hurt and betrayal. The key is choosing to move forward.

Seventy Times Seven

It is important for us to understand that people aren't perfect. Everyone knows this mentally, but it's a totally different animal to understand this *spiritually*. Earlier we stated that accusation is the nature of Satan. This would imply that offense is always the outcome the enemy intends. The Bible tells us to give him no place. The Bible goes further to say that if any have a quarrel against any, even as Christ has forgiven us, so also must we forgive others. There is no other way to heal than to forgive.

**WHEN YOU HOLD ONTO UNFORGIVENESS,
THE ONLY PERSON YOU'RE HURTING IS YOURSELF.**

We often think that forgiveness is contingent upon the actions of others, but this is absolutely false! The Bible says that while we were yet sinners, Christ died for us. (See Romans 5:8.) He forgave us before we ever acknowledged our sins. In order for us to *receive* forgiveness we must repent, but forgiveness was *extended* to us as an act of God's grace alone. Why is this important? The Bible says that we are to forgive as Christ forgave us. The last act of our Lord on the cross was to say, "Oh Father, forgive them, for they know not what they do." (See Luke 23:34.)

You may say to me, "I can't forgive!", but when you hold onto unforgiveness, the only person you're hurting is yourself. Many believers are being tormented by the enemy because they refuse to forgive. In fact, we were holding a healing service and many people were struggling with physical infirmities in their bodies. Some of them were struggling with arthritis, others were struggling with fibromyalgia, and others with Crohn's disease. They loved God and were people of faith, but they could not seem to obtain the healing.

As I began to pray for them, the Holy Spirit revealed to me that the culprit behind their affliction was offense. The vast majority of these offenses took place in the church. Some were even offended by their pastors. These precious people had opened their hearts to offenses, and thus had opened their physical bodies to infirmities. The Lord instructed me to lead the people through a prayer of repentance and forgiveness for harboring offenses. Would you believe that people began to receive physical healing instantly? Arthritis was healed. Fibromyalgia was healed. Multiple sclerosis was healed!

The Scripture tells us that as the times get darker one of the signs of the times is offense. (See Matthew 24:10.) Peoples' hearts will grow cold; there will be divisions and hurt. Look at our nation. In 2015, it took a shooting in Charleston, South Carolina, for people of different ethnic groups and backgrounds to come together and pray together. It's because there is spirit of division in the land. It's a sign of the times we're living in. But, if we grab hold of God's Word, we can live above offense. We can live and work and *love* above it.

For far too long the church has received cues from pop culture rather than being the standard-bearer for society. No longer can we allow the world to dictate to us how we ought to think and live! Let's join in a clarion call for the church to rise up and to be what God has always called us to be in the first place. It doesn't matter what's going on in the White House, it only matters what's going on in the house of God. *That's* what will determine the fate of society—not the president, not the vice-president, not the secretary of state, not the speaker of the house but the children of God in the house of God because the Bible says that *that* is the pillar and ground of the truth.

Ten Characteristics of a Kingdom Church

We often talk about what is wrong with the church, but very few people know what the church is supposed to look like. Until we understand the spiritual blueprint for the church, we will continue in frustration over the apparent flaws we behold. If you are looking for a church, or wondering whether to commit to a church that you are visiting, you may be asking, *How do I know if this is the right one for me and my family?* The answer is that there is never "the one"; every church will be imperfect! However, if the church is a kingdom church, it will be a blessing to you and you will be a blessing to it. Here are ten characteristics of a kingdom church:

1. There is a New Testament culture of empowerment and equipping all the saints to do the work of ministry. People are encouraged to participate in their own spiritual growth and development. In a kingdom church, spiritual gifts are identified, activated, and celebrated.

2. Kingdom churches are non-territorial and non-competitive. Leadership does not build confidence by demeaning other churches and leaders, but by strategic partnerships that accentuate the value of other ministries and leaders. Kingdom churches and leaders don't compete for members but birth sons and daughters through evangelism and discipleship.

3. The glory of God is made manifest through an atmosphere of worship, faith, honor, and love. The presence of God is the highest pursuit; healing, restoration, and the advancement of God's kingdom is the result.

4. The unadulterated gospel is preached with signs and wonders following. There is an authentic demonstration of the power of God that is evident through the lives of the shepherd and sheep alike.

5. There is a strong emphasis on people being *transformed* rather than just *performing* religious roles and responsibilities within a hierarchal system. People are more than numbers; they are essential components to a living spiritual community. The focus is not on activities, but on becoming actively engaged sons and daughters.

6. There is a biblical system of accountability based on a genuine desire to please God rather than manipulation and control based on insecurity. People are held accountable based on the standards of discipleship set forth in the Word of God.

7. There is an atmosphere of diversity, both culturally and ethnically. If everyone in the church looks exactly like you, there is an incongruence between the message believed and the message proclaimed. The kingdom reflects every nation, tribe, and tongue. Growth and maturity are evident, both qualitatively and quantitatively.

8. People are encouraged to become impactful in their sphere of influence. This expands the reach of the message beyond the four walls of the church building. Kingdom churches impact nations.

9. The primary goal is to build people rather than infrastructures. The infrastructure is only seen as a means to house the vision and mature believers. The announcements from the front are not all about asking for

money for the next project, they are also about inviting people to opportunities for spiritual growth.

10. Selfish ambition, pride, and gossip are strongly discouraged because they create a toxic environment that disempowers the believer and stagnates spiritual growth. Instead, there is a strong focus on mutual encouragement, edification, and truth.

This is by no means an exhaustive list of attributes, but rather a guide to help you identify the characteristics that will aid in your spiritual growth as a believer. Remember also that the church is not just about your spiritual growth but about the advancement of the kingdom of God within the community, both locally and globally. Once you commit to a church, the best question to ask yourself is not "How can the church serve my needs?" but rather, "How can I serve the needs of the church?"

THE BEST QUESTION TO ASK YOURSELF IS NOT "HOW CAN THE CHURCH SERVE MY NEEDS?" BUT RATHER, "HOW CAN I SERVE THE NEEDS OF THE CHURCH?"

The Power of Blessing

The Bible tells us in the book of Ephesians that we are blessed with all spiritual blessings in heavenly places in Christ Jesus. The writer of Ephesians uses a very interesting Greek word: it is the word *eulogia*, which means *an oral blessing*. This is where we derive the English word *eulogy*. A eulogy is a blessing spoken about a person at their funeral. It is an announcement of their good qualities, character, and attributes.

In a sense, God has eulogized us. He has spoken an oral birthright blessing over His children. One of the keys to walking in healing and holding wholeness is speaking the blessing. Slander is a curse. Gossip is a curse. These things do not originate from the heart of God, but flow from the wicked heart of the Accuser himself. Like King Balak, Satan desires to curse the children of God and seeks to use Christians to do his dirty work.

The key to lasting freedom and healing is the power of the blessing. Instead of rehearsing your pain, speak the blessing. Rather than wallowing in bitterness and defeat, speak the blessing. In doing so you are releasing God's supernatural power to heal and restore. Tell yourself how blessed you are. Tell yourself how loved you are. Tell yourself how powerful you are in Christ. Speak truth. You are more than a conqueror. You are a child of the Most High. You are healed and delivered by the stripes of Jesus Christ. You will never live in bondage again.

SATAN'S LIE: YOU CAN'T DO ANYTHING WITH YOUR SITUATION.
#HEALINGTHEWOUNDS

It is time for the church to recognize that the Accuser of the brethren is our enemy. It is time for us to rip the mask off of his sinister plot to destroy the church from the inside out. It is time for us to put on the armor of light and be the illumination that this dark world needs. What would the church look like if we actually walked in love one toward one another? How many people would be healed if we learned to say *no* to gossip, slander, and offense? How many of our fallen brothers and sisters would be restored if we learned to speak a blessing rather than the curse?

God has set before us life and death.

Brothers and sisters, now is the time to *choose life!*

The Hearts of the Fathers

God's plan is to restore His church. His whole plan is restoration! God the Father desires to restore marriages, family relationships, godly friendships, and communities. This all starts with His restoration of our souls, as referenced in Psalm 23, which begins with salvation. When our soul is restored, our life is restored.

"And he shall turn the heart of the fathers to the children, and the heart of the children to their fathers" (Malachi 4:6). This is such an amazing Scripture. It's directly talking about the Word of God, through the preaching of the second Elijah, turning hearts to their original,

intended state: oriented toward God and toward each other. This absolutely remains relevant and essential for the world today. Believers often struggle in their relationships with each other because of the state of their relationship *with God*. Is your heart turned toward God, your heavenly Father? Or has your attitude been, "Yeah, that's my Father but...." Have you really considered how important it is to be in tune with Him, and how being in tune with Him affects all of your relationships?

THERE IS NO CHRISTIANITY WITHOUT COMMUNITY.

Now, some may disagree and say "My relationship with God is good; it has nothing to do with my relationships with people," or even, "I have the Lord and I don't need anyone else." There is no way either of those statements are true. Why? Because the ministry that has been given to each one of us is all about connection. Our connection with the Father enables us to genuinely connect with other people, *especially* other believers.

Let's take a moment to look at the role of the father in a family as an example. Naturally, one of the key roles for fathers is to build the family; for this reason, God desires the father to be the head of the family. Fathers also represent strength and stability. Now, I am not saying families are devoid of these things if the father is not in the picture, because mothers are vital and amazing! Yet, God's model for the family is for both fathers and mothers to embody, illustrate, and fulfill specific roles in the lives of the children.

How does this relate to the church? A healthy, thriving relationship with the Father, God, fosters a healthy, thriving body of believers. It is said that seventy-five percent of a child's development can be attributed to the presence of the father in the home. This applies on both an individual and collective level for every single believer and therefore every single church family. At Grace & Peace Global Fellowship, we deliberately create opportunities for connecting with one another, from a time of greeting and hugging each time we come together at church, to House of Grace, our regular cell group meetings. Any church is only possible when we do things the way God says to do them, treat each other the way God says to do so, and follow the leading of the Holy Spirit, which always confirms the words God has already spoken. Galatians 3:26 says, *"for in Christ Jesus you are all sons of God, through faith"* (ESV). The body of Christ is *not* illegitimate; we *are* sons and daughters of the Most High.

When our hearts are always facing the Lord, they are also always open to others. I believe that God is raising up a generation of fathers who will restore the hearts of sons and daughters. This is the next great move of the Spirit of God in the earth. Imagine a company of sons and daughters who embrace their identity in God, and rise up to release the kingdom in every sphere of society. The Father does not accuse us or condemn us, but instead calls us to such greatness and purpose. He longs to heal the brokenhearted and the wounded alike. Now is the time for the church to rise up and be restored. Now is the time to reject slander, gossip, and offense because they are not of the Father. Now is the time to experience healing and wholeness in our hearts, so that we can fulfill the Great Commission!

For Discussion

1. What can we learn about our own healing process from the story of the man at the pool of Bethesda?

2. How can you speak blessing into your life?

3. What are some of the ways you can and will apply kingdom characteristics to your life, beginning today?

Practicum

1. Has your heart been broken by wounds of the past? Do you desire to be made whole? Declare that today is your day of healing, deliverance, restoration, and wholeness! Ask for forgiveness and show forgiveness where God reveals to you the need.

2. Have you ever considered what you look for in a church? Even if you are happily part of church, make a list of what's important for you in a church, using this chapter as reference.

3. Describe how your relationship with God, your heavenly Father, compares to/contrasts with your relationship with your earthly father. In what ways have both of those relationships affected you and the way you relate to other people? Based on what you have read in this book, think about how God truly feels about you, what He thinks and says about you, and how much He always has and always will love you. Ask God to continue molding you, like clay, into His image, so that His love, not offense, dictates your speech and actions. How can you seek restoration in your life?

Testimony

> When I first came to Grace & Peace Global Fellowship, I didn't really know my place. I was involved in ministry before, but had become disillusioned with the whole thing. After sitting under the teaching and receiving the training that I needed, I began to experience healing and restoration. Now I can walk in by gifting with confidence and joy, knowing that God loves me, and that I am able to walk in victory.
> —*Kathy*

Prayer

Father, in the name of Jesus, I thank You for who You are and all that You have done in my life. I thank You that Your Word will never return void, but it will accomplish what You have purposed it to do. You desire for me to walk in wholeness. You desire for me to experience Your healing power in every area of my life. Today I choose to freely forgive all those who have wounded me. I choose to let go of the wounds of the past and to walk in Your purpose for my life. Like the man at the pool of Bethesda, I will rise up, take up my bed, and walk. I realize today that my destiny is more powerful than my pain. My purpose is greater than my problems.

From this day forward, I walk in the blessing of the Lord that makes rich and adds no sorrow to my life. In the precious name of Jesus, I pray.

Amen!

ABOUT THE AUTHOR

Dr. Kynan T. Bridges is the senior pastor of Grace & Peace Global Fellowship in Tampa, Florida. With a profound revelation of the Word of God and a dynamic teaching ministry, Dr. Bridges has revolutionized the lives of many in the body of Christ. Through his practical approach to applying the deep truths of the Word of God, he reveals the authority and identity of the new covenant believer.

God has placed on Dr. Bridges a peculiar anointing for understanding and teaching the Scriptures, along with the gifts of prophecy and healing. Dr. Bridges and his wife, Gloria, through an apostolic anointing, are committed to equipping the body of Christ to live in the supernatural every day and to fulfill the Great Commission. It is the desire of Dr. Bridges to see the nations transformed by the unconditional love of God.

A highly sought speaker and published author of several books, including *Kingdom Authority* (Whitaker House, 2015) and *The Power of Prophetic Prayer* (Whitaker House, 2016), Dr. Bridges is also a committed husband, a mentor, and a father of four beautiful children: Ella, Naomi, Isaac, and Israel.

Welcome to Our House!

We Have a Special Gift for You

It is our privilege and pleasure to share in your love of Christian books. We are committed to bringing you authors and books that feed, challenge, and enrich your faith.

To show our appreciation, we invite you to sign up to receive a specially selected **Reader Appreciation Gift,** with our compliments. Just go to the Web address at the bottom of this page.

God bless you as you seek a deeper walk with Him!

WE HAVE A GIFT FOR YOU. VISIT:

whpub.me/nonfictionthx

WHITAKER
HOUSE